The Barmen Theses
Then and Now

The Barmen Theses
Then and Now

*The 2004 Warfield Lectures
at Princeton Theological Seminary*

Eberhard Busch

Foreword by

Daniel Migliore

Translated and Annotated by

Darrell and Judith Guder

WILLIAM B. EERDMANS PUBLISHING COMPANY

GRAND RAPIDS, MICHIGAN / CAMBRIDGE, U.K.

Originally published in German under the title
Die Barmer Thesen 1934-2004 by Vandenhoeck & Ruprecht, 2004.

This English edition published 2010 by
Wm. B. Eerdmans Publishing Co.
2140 Oak Industrial Drive N.E., Grand Rapids, Michigan 49505 /
P.O. Box 163, Cambridge CB3 9PU U.K.

Printed in the United States of America

16 15 14 13 12 11   7 6 5 4 3 2

Library of Congress Cataloging-in-Publication Data

Busch, Eberhard, 1937-
[Barmer Thesen 1934-2004. English]
The Barmen theses then and now: the 2004 Warfield lectures at
Princeton Theological Seminary / Eberhard Busch; foreword by Daniel Migliore;
translated and annotated by Darrell and Judith Guder.
p.   cm.
"Originally presented as the Warfield Lectures at Princeton Theological Seminary in 2004
. . . subsequent to the lectureship, Professor Busch revised the content and published it as
Die Barmer Thesen 1934-2004 (Göttingen: Vandenhoeck & Ruprecht, 2004).
The English translation, which had been prepared for the delivery
of the lectures at Princeton,
has been reworked to conform with the German publication" — Foreword.
Includes bibliographical references.
ISBN 978-0-8028-6617-2 (pbk.: alk. paper)
1. Barmer Theologische Erklärung.
2. Protestant churches — Germany — Doctrines — History — 20th century.
3. Creeds — Germany — History and criticism.
I. Guder, Darrell L., 1939- II. Guder, Judith J. III. Title.

BX4844.B87 2010
230′.04409430904 — dc22
2010034599

www.eerdmans.com

Contents

Foreword

Eberhard Busch is a widely respected Reformed theologian who is perhaps best-known in the English-language theological world for his volume *Karl Barth: His Life from Letters and Autobiographical Texts* (Philadelphia: Fortress, 1976). While this work will undoubtedly remain the authoritative resource on Barth's life for many years to come, Busch is far more than a biographer. He is a distinguished theologian in his own right who has authored numerous books and articles and has lectured in many countries of the world. The present volume contains a revised and enlarged version of his Warfield Lectures on the Barmen Declaration given at Princeton Theological Seminary in March 2004.

Born in 1937, Busch studied at the universities of Wuppertal, Göttingen, Heidelberg, Münster, and Basel. He inherited an interest in Barth from his father, a pastor who had attended the Barmen Synod of the Confessing Church in 1934 and had voted for the Barmen Declaration. While a student in Basel, the young Busch heard Barth lecture on what turned out to be the final volume of his *Church Dogmatics*. He was deeply moved by Barth's penetrating mind, his distinctive theological approach, and his engaging way of teaching. When Charlotte von Kirschbaum, Barth's long-time assistant, became seriously ill, Barth called on Busch to help him. Surprised and honored, Busch accepted the invitation and worked as Barth's assistant during the last three years of his life. After serving as a pastor in Ürkheim, Switzerland, for seventeen years, Busch was appointed professor for Reformed

Theology at the University of Göttingen where he taught until his retirement in 2002.

Four features of Professor Busch's work stand out. First, he is among the world's leading interpreters of the theology of Karl Barth. His significant monographs include studies of Barth's relationship to pietism and Barth's understanding of the relationship of Christians and Jews. His introductions to Barth's theology, including *The Great Passion: Introduction to Karl Barth's Theology* (Grand Rapids: Eerdmans, 2004), and his more recent and shorter work, *Barth* (Nashville: Abingdon, 2008), are excellent entrees into the thought of the most important theologian of the modern period. In his expositions of Barth's theology, Busch aims to let Barth speak for himself rather than to trim his theology to make it less provocative and more acceptable to readers. As a theology that consistently runs "against the stream," Barth's thought was and will remain offensive to both defenders and critics of the Christian gospel, and Busch does not try to soften this fact.

At the same time, Busch presents Barth and his work as being occasionally combative but as characteristically profoundly joyful. Barth often made fun of himself and his weighty books, enjoyed life to the full, and readily honored the best of human culture, including hanging in his study a portrait of his beloved Mozart alongside one of Calvin and, as Barth liked to point out, "at the same level." The deepest source of Barth's joyfulness was, of course, the great Yes of God to humanity in Jesus Christ. In his work as an interpreter, Busch notes that Barth's primary intention was not to start a new theological school or to convert his readers into slavish followers of his own theology. Rather, it was to encourage them to become once again — or perhaps for the first time — serious students of the scriptural witness to God's reconciliation of the world in Jesus Christ. For Busch as well as for Barth, the point of theology is not to translate the gospel into an abstract system or set of principles but to attend closely to the living Word of God that repeatedly requires us, in Barth's words, "to begin again and again at the beginning." As Busch writes, "Whoever engages Barth's theology does not enter a building of ideas but embarks upon a path."

Second, Busch is a Reformed theologian with an ecumenical spirit and outlook. He has made significant contributions to Calvin studies and has written and lectured frequently on the meaning and importance of a scripturally grounded confessional theology. In his view, Reformed confessions and Reformed theology offer distinctive and rich resources for the church universal. However, far from being an uncritical confessionalist, Busch's first loyalty is to the Word of God attested in Scripture. He does not hesitate to note places where the Reformed theological tradition has either deviated from or obscured the scriptural witness. The compatibility of Busch's unabashed Reformed stance and his genuine ecumenical outlook is well exhibited in his fine exposition of the Apostles' Creed titled *Credo: Das Apostolische Glaubensbekenntnis* (Göttingen: Vandenhoeck & Ruprecht, 2003). Early in this work, he notes that despite the important differences among the various churches of divided Christianity, many of them confess their common faith by frequent use of the Apostles' Creed in worship and instruction.

Busch believes that belonging to a particular confessional tradition and affirming the one, holy, catholic, and apostolic church are not mutually exclusive. On the contrary, properly understood they go hand in hand. Thus while Busch freely acknowledges that his own Reformed heritage is evident in his exposition of the Creed, he views this not as a weakness or embarrassment, but simply as an indication that in the one faith, one baptism, and one church of the one Lord Jesus Christ there are diverse voices. The goal of the ecumenical movement is not a superinstitution in which a wooden uniformity rules, but the mutual enrichment and mutual correction that may flourish when Christians of different theological traditions pray, study, and serve together, listening to and learning from each other, and above all, listening together to the witness of Scripture.

Third, Busch writes theology in the service of the church and its mission. As was true of his mentor Barth, Busch's service as a pastor leaves its mark on his theology. Barth once said that he was especially delighted when he heard that pastors found his theological work helpful in their own preaching and pastoral responsibilities. Busch is of the same mind. As is clear from his exposition of the Barmen Declaration in the present volume, he is not interested in commending this document as part of a memorable episode of modern church history, much less as a curious museum piece. Rather, he is concerned, as he says in the first of the lectures published here, that Barmen "should remain vital in the congregations," and "become a living word anew." The Barmen Declaration serves to remind the church today that it is summoned to witness to Jesus Christ as attested in Scripture as the one Word of God in life and in death, that the church lives only by the promise and command of this living Word, that there is no sphere of life in which Jesus Christ is not Lord, and that since the church is always in need of being reformed by the Word of God, it must expect to be called to fresh repentance and new obedience again and again.

Fourth, but by no means last in importance, Busch has contributed significantly to a deeper understanding of the relationship between Christians and Jews. His monumental study of Barth's relationship to and theology of the Jews titled *Unter dem Bogen des einen Bundes: Karl Barth und die Juden 1933-1945* (Neukirchen-Vluyn: Neukirchener Verlag, 1996) awaits an English translation. In this carefully researched volume, Busch shows that for Barth, as for the Apostle Paul, God's commitment to his elect people of Israel is both unequivocal and irrevocable. Christians and Jews, far from belonging to two different "religions," stand "under the arch of the one covenant." They belong to one covenant community. Busch's understanding of the relationship of Christians and Jews is thus emphatically anti-supersessionist. That is, the Christian community does not supersede, let alone replace, the people of Israel as the elect people of God. Together, Jews and Christians are one covenant community by God's electing grace in Jesus Christ.

Busch has no illusions that we can simply repeat today all of Barth's statements on the subject of the church and Israel. Still, Busch contends that when understood in its own historical context, the witness of Barth remains an extraordinary challenge to church and theology today, and should not be dismissed by facile misunderstandings of what Barth actually said and did. Of the evidence Busch collects in his study, space allows only one incident to be recalled here. On December 10, 1933, several months before the Barmen Synod, Barth preached a sermon on Romans 15:5-13 in which he declared that Jesus was a Jew, that salvation is from the Jews, and that Jesus sees both Jews who struggle with the true God and Gentiles who are at peace with false gods as children of the living God. While some critics of Barth cite this sermon as evidence of the "Christomania" that weakened Barth's witness against the assault on the Jews, Busch argues strongly against this interpretation. Barth considered anti-Semitism "a plague," and he warned that since the God of the Jews is also the God of Christians, every attack on the Jews is at the same time an attack on the message of the free grace of God in the Jew Jesus Christ. In the present volume Busch argues that the Barmen Declaration is only properly understood when it is read against the background of Barth's theologically grounded repudiation of both the explicit anti-Semitism of the "German Christian" party and the "centrist" voice of the church that was prepared to say a yes to the Hitler regime in the political realm even as it said a no to any interference of that regime in the life of the church and its proclamation.

The exposition of the Barmen Declaration that Professor Busch offers in this volume will reward careful reading and will no doubt promote lively discussion. It is to be hoped that it will also prompt many readers to turn to other writings of Busch available in English and to look with anticipation to those in process of translation.

DANIEL L. MIGLIORE
Charles Hodge Professor
of Systematic Theology Emeritus
Princeton Theological Seminary

Translators' Notes

These lectures were originally presented as the Warfield Lectures at Princeton Theological Seminary in 2004, seventy years after the Barmen Declaration was drafted in the early years of the Third Reich. Subsequent to the lectureship, Professor Busch revised the content and published it as *Die Barmer Thesen 1934-2004* (Göttingen: Vandenhoeck & Ruprecht, 2004). The English translation, which had been prepared for the delivery of the lectures at Princeton, has been reworked to conform with the German publication.

The English text of the Barmen Declaration is taken from the *Book of Confessions* of the Presbyterian Church (U.S.A.) (Louisville: Office of the General Assembly, 1991, 8.01-8.28).

Citations from the English edition of Karl Barth's *Church Dogmatics* are abbreviated as *CD* with the volume, section, and page numbers. Page numbers from the *Kirchliche Dogmatik* are indicated with the abbreviation *KD*. When it has been necessary to revise the English translation in order to convey the author's sense more faithfully, "rev." is added to the citation.

"ET" refers to "English Translation." Where English translations of German works exist, every effort has been made to cite the original resources in their published English versions.

DARRELL AND JUDITH GUDER,
Translators

The Barmen Theological Declaration in May 1934 — Its Formulation and Significance

"I am not concerned about dogmas, but I don't tolerate a cleric who gets involved in earthly matters."[1] Adolf Hitler made that remark during lunch one day in December 1941 in his military headquarters at Wolfschanze. His hidden agenda was that the church should make itself superfluous and rot away like a gangrenous leg. Behind this statement was his opinion, with which he continued his commentary, that "the organized lie" — by which he meant the church's confession of faith — must be destroyed in such a way that the state is the absolute ruler. His first statement was not really correct, of course. Obviously the Führer *was* concerned about dogmas, albeit anti-Christian ones, and obviously he did tolerate clerics, at least those whose way of dealing with earthly matters was to applaud his will to be the absolute ruler of the state. How could that ever become a temptation for the church? It must have been in a totally confused state for a long time, if this were indeed to happen. And how could the church, once it had blundered into this situation, withdraw again from it? In the Theological Declaration of Barmen of May 31, 1934, a representative synodal assembly of delegates of the Protestant Churches in Germany recognized that it had succumbed to this temptation, and in doing so it *confessed* the one through whom it was saved from this temptation. That is the primary significance of this "Declaration." Unless one un-

---

1. Henry Picker, *Hitlers Tischgespräche* [*dtv dokumente* 524] (Stuttgart: Seewald, 1976), p. 38.

derstands this, its primary significance, one will not understand it correctly.

1. The Situation of the Evangelical Churches in Germany in 1933-1934

Over time, the concept of confession had become deeply problematic in these churches, because in them the faith was broadly reduced to introspection. But then suddenly, this term surfaced again in German Christendom and was used so widely that it soon became truly inflationary. At the beginning of 1934, the church historian Kurt Dietrich Schmidt published a volume of documents in which seventy-five texts from the previous year in Germany were collected under the title "The Confessions of the Year 1933."[2] The Barmen Declaration was written therefore in the midst of a period of seething agitation, leading to the compulsion to express oneself in the form of confessions. Not a small number of these texts were linked to the so-called "Faith Movement of German Christians." In them, the confession of faith in the triune God was rather glibly connected, even mixed in, with the confessional commitment to the German people and its special history, to its authoritarian form of state, its Führer, and its German race. This was opposed by what one might call a centrist church faction. They went through several self-designations in quick succession, so that for a while they were called the "Young Reformation Movement," and then the "Pastors Emergency Federation."

This centrist group expressed itself, for example, along the lines of the Güstrow Confession of 1933. On the one hand, they averred, "We confess Jesus Christ as the perfect eternal Word of God. . . . Therefore we reject the attempt to build the church of Jesus Christ upon another foundation than solely on the revelation of God as it is testified to in Holy Scripture." But then they stated in the same breath, "We confess that God has determined the fate of ethnicities, and we recognize

---

2. K. D. Schmidt, *Die Bekenntnisse und grundsätzlichen Äusserungen zur Kirchenfrage des Jahres 1933* (Göttingen: Vandenhoeck & Ruprecht, 1934).

God's leading in the ethnocentric renewal of our fatherland" — referring to what was going on at that time! Thus, they continued, "We place ourselves in total love at the responsible service of the nation for which we are prepared to live and to die."[3] With such an approach, the centrist church combined in its 1933 confessions a "joyful yes" to the Nazi state in the *political* realm with the proclamation of grace in *the church's* realm.[4]

In contrast with those confessions, the Barmen Declaration of May 31, 1934, was truly of a different kind. Its model was the much more comprehensive Barmen Declaration of January 4, in the same year, which was fully formulated by Karl Barth and accepted by a Reformed Synod;[5] today we may read it as a commentary on the Barmen Declaration of May 1934. The decisive accomplishment of these confessions was to *exclude* categorically any combination of the texts along the lines of those of the ecclesiastical centrists mentioned above. The remarkable thing was that the adoption of the Declaration in May 1934 took place at a free synod of the German Evangelical Church that was largely attended by representatives of that centrist grouping, that is, by those who had endorsed the linkage of a political Yes to Hitler with an ecclesiastical Yes to Christ. Now this linkage had disappeared. Sometimes even church people can make rapid progress! The fact that they were now rejecting what they shortly before had supported was externally based on the fact that the representatives of the church's center at the beginning of 1934 found themselves in a catastrophe, because it had become evident that their concept was simply impracticable without joining the slippery slope of the German Christians, which they did not want to do. It was beginning to dawn upon them that they stood now before an either/or decision. In the Theological Declaration of Barmen the decision was made. The Evangelical Church now understood and made publicly known that it did *not* stand on two pillars, partially on the Word of God and partially on another "reality," but rather it stood

3. Schmidt, *Die Bekenntnisse und grundsätzlichen Äusserungen,* p. 89.

4. See "Aufruf der Jungreformatorischen Bewegung Mai 1933," in Schmidt, *Die Bekenntnisse und grundsätzlichen Äusserungen,* p. 146.

5. In: K. Barth, *Gottes Wille und unsere Wünsche, Theologische Existenz heute 7* (München: Chr. Kaiser Verlag, 1934), pp. 9-15.

only on the one rock, the Word of God. Thus the Evangelical Church existed only where this was acknowledged. Therefore confession does not mean to hold on to a confessional text that had been achieved at some earlier time in the church, while disregarding extra-ecclesial forces in its assessment. Instead, confession means to witness anew to the gospel of Jesus Christ in view of contemporary challenges. The Declaration makes this clear with its six theses. *Were* they an ecclesiastical confession? The text does not describe itself this way, but as a Theological Declaration. Be that as it may, the six theses begin with the words, "We *confess* the following evangelical truths." The church that affirmed these theses called itself thereafter the *Confessing* Church. Finally, there are other church confessions that are in force, although they do not describe themselves as such. What is more important is the question whether the Barmen Declaration could be regarded as a church confession when this Confessing Church soon thereafter ceased, for the most part, to uphold a confessional commitment to the theses of the Declaration. This much can be said: a church that no longer holds to her confession does not thereby render her confession invalid, but rather is now called to repentance by it. The worst thing would happen if, in place of such repentance, the church, with unconverted heart, would put the confession in a display case as a golden memento. It has certainly happened often enough that the church has not understood that her confession must not be left behind in a museum, but must be carried out in front of her, and she must march behind it when she moves into her battles. For the church, it is not enough to *have* a confession. She must then *live* with it.

What then makes the Barmen Declaration a confession? This will become clear when we investigate its relationship with those other German confessions from the year 1933. The Barmen Declaration is not only a confession *like* them and not only a *better* confession. It is a confession in a completely *different* way. It relates to them critically, so that it excludes and repudiates confessing in the style of 1933. How does it do this? The Barmen Declaration is, to be sure, not timeless, but it is also not time-bound as are the others. Its strength is that it guides the church in a very particular situation to listen *solely* to the Word of God, trusting it *alone,* and obeying it *alone.* This is where it differs from those other texts, for the others are listening with *one* ear to the Word of God and with the *other* to the current situation that they have already interpreted without recourse to the Word of God. The Word of God can have no other influence upon this interpretation of the situation than to approve it. One can put it this way: The 1933 texts merely *react* to the situation. Karl Barth once put it in an illuminating way — where one is reacting, "it is inevitable that our thesis should be oriented by the antithesis which is to be rejected and that by our Yes and No we keep the antithesis alive."[6] By contrast, the Barmen Declaration of 1934 stands in the service of an *action*, which is more powerful than the situation in which it is being confessed, and thus is not bound to it. As it confronts this situation, it can point to a Word that places the entire problematic of that contemporary situation within its boundaries. This is a Word that makes it possible for the church, over against earthly powers, to sing with Luther, "a little word will fell them."[7] Over against all the alleged confessions of the year 1933, the Barmen Declaration was in fact stepping into new territory, and the delegates apparently sensed this immediately, for directly after the reading of the theses, they rose from their seats and sang the chorale, "All praise and thanks to God."[8] One of the delegates spoke of a "miracle before our very eyes."[9] This reaction was picked up by the journalists present, who one day later reported on the event in the Wuppertal newspaper with the headline, "The German Synod of Confession — A Historic Event in the Church."[10] With the adoption of this text as a confession, it ceased to be merely the documentation of a theological doctrine, perhaps of a Barthian dogmatic, although it is true that Karl Barth as its primary author has the significance of an essential and remarkable commentator. But the text as such has become a *confession* of the *church* through the action of the Barmen Synod.

6. K. Barth, *KD* I/2, p. 709 = *CD* I/2, p. 633, rev.

7. The chorale "Ein feste Burg ist unser Gott," ET: "A Mighty Fortress Is Our God," verse 3.

8. In the chorale "Nun danket alle Gott," ET: "Now Thank We All Our God," verse 3.

9. *Wochenblatt "Unter dem Wort,"* June 10, 1934, according to Gerhard Niemöller, ed., *Die erste Bekenntnissynode der Deutschen Evangelischen Kirche. Texte — Dokumente — Berichte* (Göttingen: Vandenhoeck & Ruprecht, 1959), pp. 27f.

10. Reprint of the newspaper *Barmer Zeitung,* May 31, 1934.

A further indication that the Barmen Declaration was not bound to the situation in which it arose is seen in the fact that, in contrast with the so-called confessions of the year 1933, all of which have disappeared, this Declaration has been received and incorporated into their confessional traditions by churches all over the world. Even more compelling is the way that the Barmen Declaration has awakened a new joy in confession and has been one of the motivating factors for the generating of a rich variety of confessions on all continents, as Lukas Vischer has documented them.[11] It was indeed true that the Lutherans found it difficult to acknowledge the Barmen Declaration because of their view that the composition of confessions was concluded in the sixteenth century. The Reformed movement has maintained, to be sure, that new confessions can always be written. But since the eighteenth century there has also been virtually no movement of this kind among the Reformed churches. This was not because they were so delighted with the older confessions, but rather because they had come to look upon confessions in general as repugnant. And now, suddenly, Reformed, Lutheran, and United Christians were *confessing* again. Their confessing was by no means merely a position paper with regard to the error in the Protestant church at that time. Their confessing was just as much a critical engagement with the history of this church since the eighteenth century. The gradual loss of the dimension of confession indicated deep damage done to their understanding of the gospel. That damage consisted in the fact that the God of the gospel was no longer heard confronting the various worldly themes that were dominating theology — although, to be sure, they wanted to relate him to these themes. But they could not do it because he was not acknowledged to be the Lord over these themes. In Barmen this deeper damage came into view, and a conversion ensued in response to it. The susceptibility of the Evangelical Church in 1933 to National-Socialist slogans was only a symptom of that older error, the habituation to a fully wrong way of thinking. Without rejecting and leaving behind that way of thinking — without converting and transforming itself in its relation-

---

11. L. Vischer, ed., *Reformed Witness Today: A Collection of Confessions and Statements of Faith* (Bern: Evangelische Arbeitsstelle Oekumene Schweiz, 1982).

ship to the biblical God — the church could not gain any profile in its confrontations with the seductions of that time. By submitting to that conversion and making that confession in Barmen, the Evangelical Church of Germany would subsequently encourage the ecumenical church to confess. To be sure, these new confessions of the ecumenical church will need to be examined to determine whether they are taking the path of the German texts of *1933* or the path of *Barmen*. Are they listening with one ear to the Word of God while with the other they receptively listen to the historical situation without reference to this Word? Or are they listening *in* a specific situation to the Word of God *alone?*

As we said, the Barmen Declaration is not simply a Reformed confession. To be sure, it was true that the two Lutherans with whom Barth met in Frankfurt ten days before the Synod to prepare a draft of the theses took an afternoon nap while he wrote the theses alone. In so doing, he built upon theses that he had just written for the confessing fellowship in the Evangelical Church of Bonn. This made expressly clear that the subsequent confession of the entire German Confessing Church originated in a particular, local congregation. Those are blessed times, when something that happens in a particular congregation becomes a model for the entire church of Christ! This was the very text that Barth reworked during that afternoon break in Frankfurt, to produce the initial draft of the Barmen Declaration — with the result that he would later humorously describe its emergence with the words, "The Lutheran Church slept and the Reformed Church remained awake."[12] To put it more exactly, the *Lutheran* delegate Ritter stated, at the Barmen Synod in May 1934, "This text is neither confessionally Lutheran nor confessionally Reformed, but rather here the voice of the Confessing Church truly sounds, in that we acknowledge each other together."[13] The North German Reformed Church, on the other hand, would later try, after the war, to conceal the fact that it was not offi-

---

12. E. Busch, *Karl Barths Lebenslauf* (München: Chr. Kaiser Verlag, 1975), p. 258; ET: *Karl Barth: His Life from Letters and Autobiographical Texts* (Philadelphia: Fortress, 1976), p. 245.

13. E. Wolf, *Barmen. Kirche zwischen Versuchung und Gnade* (München: Chr. Kaiser Verlag, 1957), p. 75.

cially represented at Barmen. It had, at that time, concluded that it was tactically advantageous for it to align itself with the German Christian group, that is, with those against whom the Confessing Church was protesting. It excused itself with the argument that it already had an old confession and thus did not need a new one. Thus, it *possessed* a confession, but it did not actually *confess*. Certainly the church does not always need to formulate a new confession in order to be able to confess over against a concrete challenge. Its obligation, however, is to deal with its new or its old confession in such a way that, in whatever situation it is, it confesses its Lord before the people. It is not to *tend* its confession like an old banner that is unfurled occasionally on holidays but normally is preserved in a museum. That would be restoration. It must *live* with its confession, think with it, act with it. In that way it does not merely live *off of* the former Reformation, but rather lives itself *in* the Reformation. Let me probe this further.

2. The Church Confronted with Decision

First, Ernst Wolf made a proper distinction between the noun "confession" and the verb "to confess."[14] The former is an official document, whereas the latter refers to an actual event. The *confession* is a text in which the biblical witness is summarized and focused upon a particular challenge. It is formulated by a representative group in the church that speaks in the name of *the* entire church of Christ and whose Word is then ecclesiastically acknowledged. Whereas such confessions are formulated relatively seldom, *confessing* itself is a basic way of defining the daily task in the life of all Christians. The statement that they are "to confess Jesus before men" (Matt. 10:32) applies to all of them. To put it in the form of a picture: the *confessions* are guideposts on the pathway of the pilgrimage of the people of God. Certainly they also have the duty to protect this people and to warn them about errors and dead-ends. Pri-

14. E. Wolf, "Die Bindung an das Bekenntnis: Bemerkungen zu Wesen und Funktion des formulierten Bekenntnisses," in *Wort und Welt* (Berlin: Evangelische Verlagsanstalt, 1968), pp. 323-56.

marily, their positive task is to keep this people on the right path and to point the way forward. They are not the destination of that path. But they are anticipatory signs of that destination, helpful and necessary signs that point toward that destination. The verbal articulation of confessing is, so to speak, the process whereby all of the members of this people move along this path, corporately and as individuals. The church's confession does not replace but rather encourages its members' confessing. What they must actually do in practice is something they must think about again and again. The issue is to do this in the *direction* toward which the confession points. Traditionally, Lutherans emphasize more the *difference* between confession and confessing. For that reason, they are somewhat reserved about understanding the Barmen Declaration to be at the level of the Reformation confession. The Reformed emphasize more the *connection* between confession and confessing. They are thus more open to the formulation of new confessions either *next* to the old ones or even *replacing* them. When both Lutherans and Reformed confessed *together* at Barmen, the Lutherans were admonishing the Reformed not to declare the *status confessionis* too quickly, and the Reformed were admonishing the Lutherans not to be too hesitant in recognizing seriously the challenge to declare a *status confessionis*. That there is no serious disagreement in this matter is disclosed by the thoroughly Reformed definition offered by the Lutheran Dietrich Bonhoeffer: The confession — like the one from Barmen — is the "decision of the church based upon its entire doctrine, to take up the struggle at a particular place."[15]

Second, a genuine church confession cannot be had without certain *rejections*. They are not the chief concern in confessing. Although the rejection might be the major motivation for a confession, its merit will be based not upon its main message being a No to something wrong but rather upon its Yes to the truth of the divine gospel. On the other hand, even if there is no rejection specifically stated in a confession, it would be poorly understood if one failed to note that a certain No is always being said, if only implicitly — that is, a No to those views

---

15. D. Bonhoeffer, "Zur Frage nach der Kirchengemeinschaft," in *Gesammelte Schriften,* ed. E. Bethge (München: Chr. Kaiser Verlag, 1965), vol. 2, p. 227.

that contradict the positive statements being made. The positive statements would not be taken seriously if one did not see that they include the serious claim that certain other statements are excluded. The *decision* made in a confession would not be truly perceived if one failed to see that it also entails *separations.* In a remarkable way, this aspect is expressed in the Barmen Declaration from three different perspectives. First, before the text concludes with the statement that the Word of God remains in eternity, all those "whom it concerns" are asked "to return to the unity of faith, love and hope." This alleges that those who dissent from the confession no longer stand upon the ground of the church of Jesus Christ, but have in substance departed from it. This allegation is, however, not an autonomous proposition. Rather, the accent lies upon the intercessory prayer that such people should return to the community. Further, there is a definite statement of rejection attached to each of the six theses of the Declaration. One should note that in these it is never particular *persons* who are rejected; it says six times, "We reject the false *doctrine.* . . ." With that, the false doctrine is separated from those persons who espouse it. That means that in these theses they are not being cast out of the church by those who believe rightly; with their false doctrine they have excluded *themselves* from the church. Inasmuch they are now *distinguished* from their false teachings, their return into the church of Christ is made possible. Finally, and most importantly, the statement is made in the introduction that the confessors "have been given a common message," "in a time of *common need and temptation.*" This suggests that the church's confession is also a churchly *act of repentance.* In this act, it is not simply *others* inside or outside the church who are called to repentance and conversion, but rather the confessors *themselves* know that this call applies to them. At this point one sees clearly the difference between this confession and fundamentalist confessions of our day in which generally the accusing finger is pointed at others and not at one's own breast. In contrast with them, it must be said that only the truly repentant can be genuine confessors, just as proper confessors can only speak repentantly — and precisely in this way they will be enabled to speak courageously and uprightly.

Third, confessing also means *binding,* the binding of the church and of its members, not initially and decisively to the actual wording of a text drafted by the church, but rather a binding to the God who is confessed in this text. Confessing means a *new* binding of the church threatened by or already guilty of unfaithfulness, a binding to the One who gives the church its life and without whom it would cease to be the church. At stake is a new binding of the church to the one God "as he is attested for us in Holy Scripture," as it is put in the first Barmen thesis. What this demonstrates is not the merely asserted but the real and proper binding of the church, which is that its confession of God is at the same time its binding to Holy Scripture. It is not thereby bound to any number of individual truths to be found in the Bible but rather it is bound to the *one* authoritative truth proclaimed in Scripture, which, to be sure, is made radiantly clear in particular texts. Paul speaks in 2 Corinthians 9:13 of "your obedience in confessing the gospel of Christ." This accords with Barth's view that one will always recognize the community's confession in that it is "the voice of *students* (of Holy Scripture) who as such are not to recount something of their own making — not even something Christian, something that they have fashioned out of the Bible — but rather, each in his own manner and speech, is to recount what they have all *learned* together in that school."[16] For that reason the church's confessions do not stand next to, certainly never above, but always *under* Scripture, so that every confession is to be read on the basis of Scripture, and not Scripture on the basis of a confession. The Barmen Declaration makes this clear in an impressive way. At a time in which the church had been invaded by the arbitrariness of human views and interpretations, it was a necessary aspect of Christian confession that all six theses begin with direct citations from Scripture. These citations make clear how indispensably necessary it had become, in view of the confusing lack of clarity at that time, for the church to say *from which source* it derived its decisions, positions, and imperatives. Therefore, these citations are not mere introductions to the "actual" confession, and they are not mere proof-texts for someone's opinion. They are themselves the community's confession. One may assume that the authoritative rank assigned to Scripture, signaled in this fashion, is what

16. K. Barth, *KD* III/4, p. 91 = *CD* III/4, p. 83 rev.

led the various parties — the Reformed, Lutherans, and United — to make this first-ever common confession together. The Leuenberg Fellowship of Evangelical Churches in Europe, founded in 1973, has one of its sources here. The Barmen Declaration not only made visible the *separation* from a false church. It also proved at the same time to be a significant *bridge* connecting churches that had long been separated. That is its ecumenical significance. It demonstrates that where the church attempts to speak in the name of God *in a binding way,* this results in new *bonds.* To put it in the words of the Confession of 1967 of the United Presbyterian Church in the U.S.A., "Obedience to Jesus Christ alone identifies the one universal church. . . ."[17]

3. The Beginning of the Barmen Theological Declaration

The six theses that form the substance of the Declaration are preceded by a long introduction. Here, initially, the first two articles of the constitution of the German Evangelical Church are cited, which makes clear that what follows wants to be understood as stated in the name of this church. A passage then follows explaining why this church is now uttering a word of confession. This passage is cited here in three sections and commented upon.

> *We, the representatives of Lutheran, Reformed, and United Churches, of free synods, church assemblies, and parish organizations united in the Confessional Synod of the German Evangelical Church, declare that we stand together on the ground of the German Evangelical Church as a federation of German Confessional churches. We are bound together by the confession of the one Lord of the one, holy, catholic, and apostolic church.*

"We are bound together by the *confession* of the one Lord of the one, holy, catholic, and apostolic church." Confessing — both in its substantive form (confession) and in its verbal form (confessing) — is

17. L. Vischer, *Reformed Witness Today* (see note 11), p. 159; *Book of Confessions,* 9.03, 253.

the activity in which Christians *express outwardly* their faith. Their confessing is no mere possible consequence of faith but is the self-evident form of faith itself. Believing and confessing belong together. Confessing belongs as definitively to their believing as, to cite Jesus' words, one lights a candle not to conceal it but so that the entire house may be illumined (Matt. 5:15). Paul says in Romans 10:9, "If you confess with your *lips* that Jesus is Lord and believe in your *heart* that God raised him from the dead, you will be saved." One only believes as much in one's heart as what comes across one's lips. Therefore, Calvin said, "If you don't want to *confess* yourself as a Christian, you cannot be taken to be a Christian."[18] If Christian faith is faith *in Jesus Christ,* then confessing is confessing *Jesus Christ.* In their confessing, Christians *express their commitment* to their *Lord.* According to Matthew 10:32, confessing means "to acknowledge *him* before men." In their bond to him they did not first bind themselves to him. He has bound himself to us so very much that he is prepared to acknowledge *us* before his "Father who is in heaven." In so doing, he has bound us to himself and to his heavenly Father. However diverse and even divided Christians might be, what binds them together into one, holy, catholic, and apostolic church is their confession of *this* Lord of the church. If they are bound together *through him,* they are then led by that to their confession *of him.*

> *We publicly declare before all evangelical churches in Germany that what they hold in common in this Confession is grievously imperiled, and with it the unity of the German Evangelical Church. It is threatened by the teaching methods and actions of the ruling church party of the "German Christians" and of the church administration carried on by them. These have become more and more apparent during the first year of the existence of the German Evangelical Church. This threat consists in the fact that the theological basis, in which the German Evangelical Church is united, has been continually and systematically thwarted and rendered ineffective by alien principles on the part of the leaders and spokesmen of the "German Christians" as well as on the*

18. J. Calvin, *Catechism of Geneva* (1545), Question 363.

part of the church administration. When these principles are held to be valid, then, according to all the Confessions in force among us, the church ceases to be the church and the German Evangelical Church, as a federation of Confessional churches, becomes intrinsically impossible.

As members of Lutheran, Reformed, and United Churches, we may and must speak with one voice in this matter today. Precisely because we want to be and to remain faithful to our various Confessions, we may not keep silent, since we believe that we have been given a common message to utter in a time of common need and temptation. We commend to God what this may mean for the interrelations of the Confessional churches.

These sentences declare how the confessional statement came to be. They speak "in a time of common need and temptation," in a situation in which the church is "grievously imperiled." It is imperiled because "its theological basis . . . has been continually and systematically thwarted and rendered ineffective by alien principles." If one views this spiritually and thus exactly, then the following confessional statements did not come about because a "better part" of the church had triumphally asserted itself against a "problematic part." The church that is speaking here has participated in this grievous imperiling of the church. It did so because it did not comprehend that the outcome of what the German Christians sought was the church's ceasing "to be the church." By failing to recognize this, it would itself also stand outside the church of Jesus Christ. The Barmen Declaration takes this insight so seriously that it says that this church cannot liberate itself from this jeopardy, but it was being liberated; it *"has been given a common message to utter* in a time of common need and temptation." This wording is reminiscent of 2 Chronicles 20:12, where Israel in its distress prays, "We do not know what to do, but our eyes are upon you." Or also Romans 8:26: "We do not know how to pray as we ought, but the Spirit himself intercedes for us." Above all, the words from the calling of Jeremiah to be a prophet echo here, when God speaks to him even as he is resisting his calling: "Behold, I have put my words in your mouth" (Jer. 1:9). In such a way those who are not fit to confess are made into confessors.

In view of the errors of the "German Christians" of the present Reich Church government which are devastating the church and are also thereby breaking up the unity of the German Evangelical Church, we confess the following evangelical truths.

In this confessional commitment to God, diverse persons are bound to each other to form a fellowship of confessors of the One who is the ground of their faith, of their hope, and of their love. They are so bound to each other that they cannot be Christians in isolation but only together with others. They are bound to God in such a way that even old divisions among Christians can be overcome. Although certainly their diverse traditions need not be surrendered as they are now brought together, these traditions lose their character as an expression of their separation. What binds these diverse people to each other is the fact that Christ is the head through which they are members of his body — while still remaining very different members. And because they have this one head, they are vitally connected to each other in the manifold differences of many members. This excludes simultaneously both individualism and collectivism — an individualism in which each one corresponds to the other by the fact that all live in profound isolation, and a collectivism in which each one is so similar to the other that no one is allowed to be who he or she really is. If the community of Christ does not bear the name of Christ in vain, then it lives beyond both of these dangers. Each one in his or her distinctiveness is then what matters. And the church lives in a fellowship of participation and cooperation. In the church's bonds to the one head of the community no single member is disqualified, but rather all are taken seriously as qualified and responsible. In this community under this one head, all members have a commission, *this* commission: to confess Christ before the people. But the variety of gifts, of charisms, expresses itself in the way that this confession of Christ takes place in a multiplicity of *different* ways. It should not be forgotten that it happens in an especially prominent way in the form of confession with the lips. There are special situations in life in which if there is no clear speech then there is no appropriate action either.

4. Texts Relating to the Barmen Declaration

The Declaration is the word of confession of God, spoken in a particular situation and challenge, which the Christian church confesses at all times and in all places. As such it has received ecclesiastical acknowledgment beyond the context of that particular period and situation. The Evangelical Church in Germany and its member churches, the Evangelical Churches of the Augsburg and Helvetic Confessions in Austria as well as the Church of the Augsburg Confession and the Reformed Church in Alsace and Lorraine "see the Barmen Theological Declaration as an important document from the period of the Church Struggle. Their consensus is that it serves as a witness for faith and doctrine which guides the church in the twentieth century. Not a few attribute to it obligatory significance, and a few recognize it as part of their confessional basis (the Evangelical-Reformed Church, the Evangelical Church of the Union)."[19] "It continues to be recognized as a scripturally faithful and obligatory testimony to the Gospel for the ministry of the church."[20] The Evangelical Church in Germany (EKD) declared in 1938, "Together with its member churches, it [the EKD] affirms the decisions made at the first Confessional Synod in Barmen. It recognizes its obligation as confessing church to implement the insights of the Church Struggle regarding the essence, the commission and the order of the church. It calls upon the member churches to listen to the witness of the brothers. It helps them, where it is required, to resist together heresies that destroy the churches."[21] The Barmen Declaration has also been acknowledged as a basic ecclesiastical confession beyond the boundaries of Europe, as for example by the United Presbyterian Church in the USA, in Canada, and in Cuba. All of this demonstrates that this text adopted in May 1934 by representatives of the Lutheran, Re-

19. *Evangelisches Gesangbuch. Ausgabe für die Evangelisch-Lutherische Kirche in Niedersachsen und für die Bremische Kirche,* Nr. 809.

20. *Evangelisches Gesangbuch für die Evangelische Kirche im Rheinland, in Westfalen, Lippe und für die Evangelisch-Reformierte Kirche,* Nr. 858.

21. A. Burgsmüller and R. Weth, eds., *Die Barmer Theologische Erklärung: Einführung und Dokumentation* (Neukirchen-Vluyn: Neukirchener Verlag, 1983), pp. 71f.

formed, and United Churches is not restricted to that time but is relevant and meaningful today outside the setting of Germany.

There is by now a well-developed literature for the research and study of this text, which I will survey briefly. The original text is accessible in the hymnals of the various German provincial churches and in the resource edited by Alfred Burgsmüller and Rudolf Weth titled *Die Barmer Theologische Erklärung: Einführung und Dokumentation* (Neukirchen-Vluyn, 1985); the second edition has a foreword by Eduard Lohse, while Klaus Engelhardt provided the foreword for the fifth edition (1993).[22] The fifth edition also contains Hans Asmussen's introduction of the text given at the Barmen Synod. The following publications are used as *resources* for the church history of that period: Kurt Dietrich Schmidt, ed., *Die Bekenntnisse und grundsätzlichen Äusserungen zur Kirchenfrage des Jahres 1933* (Göttingen, 1934); Kurt Dietrich Schmidt, ed., *Die Bekenntnisse und grundsätzlichen Äusserungen zur Kirchenfrage des Jahres 1934*, vol. 2 (Göttingen, 1935); and Joachim Gauger, *Chronik der Kirchenwirren*, 3 vols. (Elberfeld, 1934-1935). Important for the reconstruction of the actual *emergence* of the Barmen text: Christoph Barth, *Bekenntnis im Werden: Neue Quellen zur Entstehung der Barmer Erklärung* (Neukirchen-Vluyn, 1979); Carsten Nicolaisen, *Der Weg nach Barmen: Die Entstehungsgeschichte der Theologischen Erklärung von 1934* (Neukirchen-Vluyn, 1985); Gerhard Niemöller, *Die erste Bekenntnissynode der Deutschen Evangelischen Kirche in Barmen; I: Geschichte, Kritik und Bedeutung der Synode und ihrer Theologischen Erklärung, II: Text — Dokumente — Berichte* [Arbeiten zur Geschichte des Kirchenkampfes, vols. 5-6] (Göttingen, 1959). Of the *interpretations* of the Declaration, I mention these: Karl Barth, *Texte zur Barmer Theologischen Eklärung*, introduced by Eberhard Jüngel, edited by Martin Rohkrämer (Zürich, 1984); Ernst Wolf, *Barmen: Kirche zwischen Versuchung und Gnade* (Munich, 1957 — a discussion with critics of the text). The most comprehensive and important expositions of the Declaration have been published by the Theologische Kommission of the Evangelische Kirche der Union: Wilhelm Hüffmeier, ed., *Das eine Wort Gottes — Botschaft für alle, I: Vorträge aus dem Theologischen Ausschuss*

22. Both Lohse and Engelhardt were bishops of member churches of the EKD and served as Presidents of the Evangelical Church in Germany — TR.

der Evangelischen Kirche der Union zu Barmen I und VI, II: Votum des Theologischen Ausschusses der Evangelischen Kirche der Union (Gütersloh, 1994, 1993); Alfred Burgsmüller, ed., *Zum politischen Auftrag der christlichen Gemeinde (Barmen II)* (Gütersloh, 1984); Alfred Burgsmüller, ed., *Kirche als "Gemeinde von Brüdern" (Barmen III)*, 2nd ed. (Gütersloh, 1981); and Wilhelm Hüffmeier, ed., *Für Recht und Frieden sorgen: Auftrag der Kirche und Aufgabe des Staates nach Barmen V; Theologisches Votum der Evangelischen Kirche der Union*, 2nd ed. (Gütersloh, 1986).

The following discussion of the Barmen Declaration presupposes this literature and works with it. The purpose guiding this effort is a special one. This is an attempt to explain *what* is actually being said by the way that the text of 1934 speaks as its does. I want to address with all seriousness the fact that what was said *then* continues to speak to us today after seventy years, and that this is not an accident but rather because the *church* spoke in what was said then. The church hears this confessional word in its historical setting, but also in contact with church utterances of earlier ages and in the conviction that this word also speaks to us and with us. It will become clear to the reader that the author is of the Reformed confession. The exposition is open for the possibility that adherents of the Lutheran confession will read the text with *their* eyes and *their* understanding. Be that as it may, it should not be forgotten that in Barmen Lutheran, Reformed, and United Christians made a *common* confession. In the process of the exposition, it is the intention to present the Declaration in such a way that it will be understandable and accessible to interested congregational members. If I am not mistaken, this is important today in new ways. The Barmen Declaration was an endeavor that was related to the congregations. Of what help or use is its understanding as a confession or as guiding text, and of what purpose are the masses of documentation and scientific debates relating to this Declaration, if it is not that the fundamental word of the Confessing Church should remain vital in the congregations or become a living word anew?

Jesus Christ as the One Word of God and the Jews as the Elect People of God

Thesis 1: "I am the way, and the truth, and the life; no one comes to the Father, except through me" (John 14:6). "Very truly, I tell you, anyone who does not enter the sheepfold by the gate but climbs in by another way is a thief and a murderer. . . . I am the gate. Whoever enters by me will be saved" (John 10:1, 9).

Jesus Christ, as he is attested for us in Holy Scripture, is the one Word of God which we have to hear and which we have to trust and obey in life and in death.

We reject the false doctrine, as though the church could and would have to acknowledge as a source of its proclamation, apart from and besides this one Word of God, still other events and powers, figures and truths, as God's revelation.

"The beginning is half of the whole," is a principle of the ancient philosopher Aristotle.[1] By this he meant that decisions made in the beginning determine everything that follows. But, what is the *right* first step? The playwright Goethe wrote in *Faust*: "'In the beginning was the *word*'? Here I falter already! It is impossible for me to value the word so highly. I have to translate it in another way . . . and write confidently: In the beginning was the *deed*."[2] What is the word and what the deed, if

---

1. Aristotle, *Politeia*, V, 4; ET: Aristotle, *Politics*, trans. B. Jowett (New York: Random House, 1943), V, 4, p. 217.

2. J. W. von Goethe, *Faust*, vv. 1224-26, 1236f.

19

such a distinction is made between them? The deed must not necessarily be the opposite of what the Holy Scripture does, in fact, assert: "In the beginning was the *word*" (John 1:1). And the first thesis of Barmen begins with *this* beginning. Its decisive statement is this: "Jesus Christ . . . is the one Word of God." I would like to exposit this statement in the context of the whole thesis and then inquire about its relationship to the knowledge of the divine election of the people of Israel.

1. Questions

I will start by mentioning the objections that have been raised against this thesis. The primary author of the theses and especially of the first one, Karl Barth, enumerated them in 1959. This statement would mean "an impoverishment of thought" in view of the plenitude of ideas that were excluded "by the demand that one of them should be declared . . . normative, and that this normativeness should be denied to all the rest." This proposition would mean "the breakdown of communication and even in the last resort of fellowship between Christians and non-Christians, and . . . it implies for its champions an unfitting . . . constriction. . . . [I]t is the proclamation of unconcealed intolerance and therefore an intolerable disruption of the co-existence of men of different outlooks and confessions, . . . and therefore the potential, and basically already actual, principle of the repression and persecution of those who think or believe differently. . . ." And Barth adds that such things are not only heard from outsiders but that "there will be in ourselves an inner voice speaking and arguing and remonstrating along these lines."[3]

This criticism of the first Barmen thesis has been raised in particular ways from the side of Judaism. According to Pinchas Lapide, the formula that speaks of Jesus Christ as the "one Word of God" strongly emphasizes what separates the church from the synagogue, and excludes from salvation all Jews who do not believe in Jesus. In this sense, Lapide says literally that the first Barmen thesis could "indirectly become the

3. K. Barth, *KD* IV/3, p. 99 = *CD* IV/3, pp. 89f.

sponsor of a social anti-Semitism, the advance preparation for racist apartheid and ultimately for genocide." For "whoever is a Jew is not a 'Christian' . . . , and thus can only be an inferior human who has as such no right to life."[4] The Bonhoeffer scholar Eberhard Bethge agrees with this when he states that, in point of fact, this thesis could be understood as "a cruel primary proposition of the Christians," which caused "punishment and suffering" for the Jews.[5] One should keep this criticism in mind, although I am not yet going to address it directly.

2. The One Word

I would like first of all to bring out, in three thoughts, the distinctive sense of this thesis, and in order to do that I will turn our attention to the period of time before the Barmen Synod.

1) One year before Barmen a circle of Reformed churchmen published the so-called Düsseldorf Theses, whose first thesis was the immediate predecessor to the first Barmen thesis. It stated, "The holy Christian Church, whose only Head is Christ, is born out of the Word of God; it remains in it and does not listen to the voice of a stranger."[6] The church does not belong to itself, for it is born out of the Word of God. This is also the statement in James 1:18 so much prized by Luther.[7] This proposition is, as a whole, a citation of the first thesis of the Reformation in the Swiss cantons of Graubünden in 1526[8] and of Bern in 1528.[9] It goes back to Huldrych Zwingli. For him this statement was a summary of the John 10 message about the good Shepherd who gives

---

4. P. Lapide, *Jeder kommt zum Vater. Barmen und die Folgen* (Neukirchen-Vluyn: Neukirchener Verlag, 1984), p. 21.

5. E. Bethge, "Christologisches Bekenntnis und Antisemitismus: Zum Defizit von Barmen I," in W. Hüffmeier and M. Stöhr, eds., *Barmer Theologische Erklärung 1934-1984* (Bielefeld: Luther Verlag, 1984), p. 57.

6. K. D. Schmidt, *Die Bekenntnisse und grundsätzlichen Äusserungen zur Kirchenfrage des Jahres 1933* (Göttingen: Vandenhoeck & Ruprecht, 1934), p. 149.

7. Cf. Martin Luther, *Leipziger Disputation,* WA 2, p. 430.

8. H. Bullinger, *Reformationsgeschichte,* ed. J. H. Hottinger and H. H. Vögeli (Frauenfeld: Beyel, 1838), vol. I, p. 315.

9. E. F. K. Müller, *Die reformierten Bekenntnisschriften* (Leipzig: Deichert, 1903), pp. 30f.

his life for his sheep and to whose voice they listen.[10] In the many weeks of disputation at the beginning of the Bern Reformation, it was the Reformers' formulation regarding Christ as the *"only* head" of the church that evoked contradiction from the so-called "old believers." When the first Düsseldorf thesis of 1933 cited this proposition from the sixteenth century, the intention was to find a formulation in which the confession of the one Head of the church would *not,* as was otherwise customary in 1933, be introduced with the praise of the National Socialist takeover of the government. When, one year later in Barmen, the Swiss Reformation's thesis was not simply repeated but instead a new formulation was attempted, one that was instructed by it, then this must be understood in a particular way. It meant that the mere quoting of an old text could not provide the needed clarity in this situation in which the church was threatened and under assault. They experienced something very important: In order to say *the same thing* that had once been said, it had to be said in a *new way.*

2) Scarcely one year before the Barmen Synod, a constitution of the German Evangelical Church was published with the official acknowledgment of the German government. In its first article, there is language that speaks of "Jesus Christ, as He is attested for us in Holy Scripture. . . ." In the introduction to the Barmen Declaration, this wording is expressly used, and the first Barmen thesis also cites it, but intensifies it with the addition of the five words, *"the one Word of God"*: "Jesus Christ, as he is attested for us in Holy Scripture, is the one Word of God." These five words must be seen as the center and the provocation of the thesis — that is, that which provokes the *church* in the situation of that time, which calls out to it to stand and not to fall, to resist and not to conform, to confess and not to remain silent. It is appropriate to make very clear at this point that the church is not trying to bolster its courage by inventing a clever slogan. One must look here at the two scriptural citations that initiate the thesis. *They* are what puts the church that listens to them on its legs again, that opens its mouth and gives it courage: John 14:6 where Jesus speaks, "I am the way, and the

---

10. Huldrych Zwingli, "Christliche Antwort an Bischof Hugo," *Zwinglis Werke,* vol. 3 (Leipzig: Deichert, 1914), p. 168, 6-10.

truth, and the life; no one comes to the Father, except through me"; and John 10:1 and 9: "Very truly, I tell you, anyone who does not enter the sheepfold by the gate but climbs in by another way is a thief and a murderer. I am the gate. Whoever enters by me will be saved." No one comes to the Father except that the Father comes to us in his Son, Jesus Christ. There is no other way and no other door to salvation. The one Word is, therefore, not one of the possibilities that people have selected among many and made into an absolute; *they* are the ones who are called thieves and murderers, those who steal the gospel and get rid of people. The one Word is the way upon which, and the door through which, God comes to us in his truth and in his life, comes as the light that overcomes the lie and as the resurrection that disempowers death. Because he comes to us as the one Word, and "was made flesh" in the wording of John 1:14, the *One* comes to us in whom truth and life are combined without contradicting each other, not truth at the expense of life and not life at the expense of truth.

3) In his first commentary on the first thesis immediately after the Barmen Synod Karl Barth said, "Why must this be said today?" Answer: Because "we really must grasp in a wholly new way what the first commandment means: I am the Lord thy God."[11] Before the Synod he had already insisted on this: "In the matter of the first commandment there is dispute in the church today, and at this time we must 'confess' it."[12] In fact, his first public statement on the Third Reich was his lecture titled "The First Commandment as Theological Axiom."[13] There, he said, "The God of the first commandment is thus the God of humanity . . . , because and in that he is the mighty and gracious God of Israel."[14] It is certainly the case that theology, in view of "its responsibility toward the first commandment, sees revelation in relation — and in its thought and speech *sets* revelation in relation — to reason, exis-

---

11. K. Barth, *Texte zur Barmer Theologischen Erklärung,* ed. M. Rohkrämer (Zürich: Theologischer Verlag, 1984), p. 18.

12. K. Barth, "Gottes Wille und unsere Wünsche," *Theologische Existenz heute* 7 (München: Chr. Kaiser Verlag, 1934), p. 6.

13. K. Barth, *Theologische Fragen und Antworten: Gesammelte Vorträge* (Zürich: Zollikon, 1957), vol. 3, pp. 127-43.

14. Barth, *Theologische Fragen,* p. 133.

tence, creation or whatever the other instances might be called, because it *must* do so." *And yet,* it depends upon the fact — to which the first commandment obligates us — that "it will interpret those other instances according to the standard of revelation and not revelation according to the standard of those other instances."[15] The reproach of "Christomonism"[16] against this thesis is based on a misunderstanding. For the pointed way in which the declaration of Jesus Christ as the *one* Word of God enters into this thesis corresponds to the pointed emphasis of the *first commandment* of Exodus 20:3. It is understood in terms of the New Testament, but in such a way that the New Testament message is heard entirely in terms of the Old Testament. For this, Matthew 6:24 must constantly resound in one's ear, where it does not say merely "you *shall* not," but rather "you *cannot* serve God and mammon," because the attempt to serve both will always mean that only *mammon,* the idol of this world, will have been served. The firmness with which "You shall and you cannot do this" is said is based on the fact that in the first commandment, in his one word, God speaks to us as the One whom *we* neither initially nor decisively distinguish from others, but who *himself* distinguishes himself from other gods.

The major clause about Jesus Christ as the one Word of God is then rendered more precise by two subordinate clauses. The first one refers to Jesus Christ, to no other one than him, and to him solely as the One who "is attested for us in Holy Scripture." Because he is as this One *alive,* there may well be manifold ways of understanding him. But they are all subject to the testimony of Holy Scripture regarding him. They are all to be guided by it, to be enriched by it, and also to be corrected by it. The German Christians made the decision in November 1933 that they wanted to purify the gospel "from all Oriental distortion."[17] With that they accomplished the very opposite — they distorted the message. There have been for a long time and there are also today tendencies to subject the figure of Jesus Christ attested to us in Scripture to the favorite ideas of a particular point in time — until we discover one day that we

15. Barth, *Theologische Fragen,* pp. 139f.

16. W. Elert; see E. Wolf, Art. "Barmen," RGG3 I, p. 877.

17. A. Burgsmüller and R. Weth, eds., *Die Barmer Theologische Erklärung: Einführung und Dokumentation* (Neukirchen-Vluyn: Neukirchener Verlag, 1983), p. 35.

can satisfy our ideals really much better without this figure! It will constantly be a Reformational act when one moves away from such fantasies to the hearing of Holy Scripture. It will give our fantasy enough to do. It is important to listen to the *entire* Holy Scripture in *both* testaments. The unity of the Word of God attests itself in the unity of the Bible. In the Barmen Declaration of January 1934 this is explained as a *differentiated* unity: "The church listens to the Word of God by the free grace of the Holy Spirit in the double and yet unified witness of the Old and New Testaments in which both [. . .] parts are mutually dependent."[18] Not just in 1933 but going back as far as Schleiermacher, the question was not whether the Old Testament was a book for the Jews but rather whether this Jewish Bible is also a book for the *church*. Christendom stood again, like the ancient church, before the central question whether the first part of its Bible is the *Old Testament* or is rather to be found in the stories of its natural ethnicities, and whether the Old Testament is to be read in contrast to the New Testament or in connection with it. The first Barmen thesis makes it fundamentally clear that Christ is attested in the *Holy Scriptures,* and thus in the Old Testament as well. One might add, as it was said then, that the Old Testament is the book of the *announcement* of the One who is coming, just as the New Testament is the *pronouncement* of the One who has come and, all the more decisively, is coming. In the way that the two testaments belong to each other and in their varying perspectives their difference is defined. If one does not attend to both, to their belonging together and their difference, the entire Bible will be wrongly understood. In the place of the Old Testament, one will make, as was done under Hitler, one's membership in some heathen culture and one's engagement in its myths into the presupposition of the New Testament, and in so doing will sin against both testaments. Then the two testaments will be understood as the witnesses of two different *religions.* By contrast, the Barmen thesis enables a new view in that it understands both testaments as belonging to the "one Word," as do the two communities documented in it.

18. "Erklärung über das rechte Verständnis der reformatorischen Bekenntnisse in der Deutschen Evangelischen Kirche der Gegenwart," *Theologische Existenz heute* 7 (München: Chr. Kaiser Verlag, 1934), p. 10.

The second subordinate clause in the first thesis explains the formulation "one Word of God." *Because* it is the *one* word, it is the word "which we have to hear and which we have to trust and obey in life and in death." The words "in life and in death" are taken from Romans 14:8 and from the first question of the Heidelberg Catechism, and they remind us of the statement made there that it is for our comfort and remembrance that we under no circumstances belong to ourselves but to our "faithful Savior Jesus Christ." Thus we can understand the statement of church-leaders in China [in 1985] that this first thesis "again and again consoled, cheered and encouraged us in the long years of isolation."[19] The three verbs, *hear, trust,* and *obey,* are a free reception of the three concepts with which traditionally the concept of "faith" has been explained. The concept "hearing" indicates that Christian existence is entirely defined by the beginning that God initiates with us. God alone connects himself to us. This renders superfluous Emil Brunner's doctrine that *we* have to bring about such a point of connection, and are capable of doing so.[20] Not only is God's *work* for us and in us pure grace, but also the fact that he makes himself knowable by us. And the other two concepts indicate *how* our existence is defined in this way; that is, in relation to the Word of God we do both — we trust and we obey. "Trusting" leaves no room for quietism as long as it is accompanied by "obeying." And act-focused obedience does not produce works-righteousness as long as it is defined by trust. In a subtle way the three verbs, *hear, trust,* and *obey,* refer to the three offices in the Old Testament, which are united in Jesus Christ as the one Word: the office of prophet, priest, and king.

3. "No" to Natural Theology

The third part of the thesis states, "We reject the false doctrine, as though the church could and would have to acknowledge as a source of its proclamation, apart from and besides this one Word of God, still

19. E. Lohse and R. Koppe, *Offene Türen: Begegnungen mit Christen in China,* GTB Siebenstern 1090 (Gütersloh: Gütersloher Verlagshaus, 1986), p. 6.
20. Cf. *Karl Barth–Emil Brunner: Briefwechsel 1916-1966,* ed. Eberhard Busch (Zürich: Theologischer Verlag, 2000), pp. 464f.

other events and powers, figures and truths, as God's revelation." What is being negated here? Karl Barth constantly put it very succinctly: this is the No to natural theology. And what is meant by that? Shortly after the Barmen Synod, he said, "This No does not deny that . . . figures, events, and powers have a certain value for our life. . . . We do not deny the proposition that God has the entire world, including such figures, events, and powers, in his hands, nor do we even deny that he also reveals himself in them."[21] Barth extensively confirmed this statement in his *Church Dogmatics* in 1959: the one true Word of God finds its echo in true creaturely words, even outside the area of the church.[22] The community of Jesus Christ must count on this, for this is not excluded by that No. Nor does this No dispute the fact that the one Word of God is a *living* Word, which constantly speaks in new ways and must be heard in new ways. Nor does it dispute the fact that God as the Creator, the Reconciler, and the One who sanctifies us, works in each instance in *different ways*.

But that No disputes that we, when we are dealing with all this liveliness and difference, are encountering *another* God from the One who has spoken in the history attested to in Holy Scripture. Here he has spoken in such a way that he has defined himself. This No disputes the idea that Christians, in their hearing, trusting, and obeying, should rely on some *other* god and his word "aside from and next to" this one God. To speak of *one* Word repudiates precisely the claim that there is a *second* word of *another* god that purports to be authoritative for the Christian witness and is thus not subject to the standard of the one Word. What distinguishes then the *one* Word from some *second* word? The term "Word of God" designates a particular story as it is "attested for us in holy Scripture." In this story God *distinguishes himself* from all other gods. By electing particular people to be his people, he differentiates himself from the gods that people choose for themselves. By carrying out this self-differentiation God makes the judgment, so infuriating to his *own* people, that all gods "aside and next to him," and especially those that the members of his people might choose for themselves, are *false* and presumptive gods. As proof that he has elected them and not they him,

---

21. K. Barth, *Texte zur Barmer Theologischen Erklärung* (see note 11), p. 19.
22. K. Barth, *KD* IV/3, pp. 107-53 = *CD* IV/3, pp. 96-135.

he does not give them up even when they turn to false gods, but reveals himself then to be their strict reconciler. Here the contrast between natural theology and the biblical God is evident. Such a theology acknowledges *something other* as god. In what way? In such a natural theology, the human spirit already has so much of the divine spirit within it that it can comprehend God by means of its own capacity to do so. It has no real need of God's coming to meet it. Thus it is only recognizing itself and what it is capable of in a magnified form. But it does not know God, the true and biblical God whom we can only know when he makes himself knowable as an act of pure grace.

But since God has differentiated himself from the gods *in such a way,* the church cannot for its part arbitrarily choose to serve God *and* mammon, that is, the worldly powers. It must constantly acknowledge God's self-differentiation from them. And it must distinguish between this God and everything else that one might acknowledge as "God's revelation" *within itself* aside from and next to God, under the impression of certain "events and powers, figures and truths." To *whom* is this No of the rejecting proposition directed? It is important to see that this statement is not a saying shouted through the window to those who are absent in order either to set oneself off from them or to win out over them; it certainly is not a word spoken against the Jews, as Lapide thinks. The statement is about an instrument that is in God's hand alone. Concretely, it is therefore *first of all* a word of repentance in which the confessors must beat their *own* breasts. There was very real cause for that repentance. For, up until then, the confessors had, to be sure, made a distinction between themselves and the German Christians at some points. But they could not articulate a fundamental distinction because basically they were thinking in the same pattern as that movement. This pattern made room, on the one hand, for faith-centered preaching for the heart, or within churchly spaces, while on the other hand, it endorsed the church's "joyful yes" to the racial nationalistic ideology.[23] This "yes" was even theologically grounded, but

---

23. "Grundsätze der Jungreformatoren, 12.5.1933," in J. Gauger, *Chronik der Kirchenwirren* (Elberfeld, 1934), p. 77. "Racial nationalistic" renders the German adjective "völkisch" — TR.

with reference to another god from the One who is "attested for us in Holy Scripture." By virtue of this wrong theological basis, the church became obliged to obey strictly this alien god in its worldly life. In fact, by doing so, the church gave theological sanction to the violation of the first commandment. Any and every attempt to combine the one Word with other entities next to and aside from it is always the surrender of our binding to the one Word of God. This is precisely what is meant by "natural theology." Now we may understand that the formula about the one Word of God is the self-critical repudiation of the attempt to serve both God *and* mammon. It is the simple and yet revolutionary decision of the church that says: In the witness that the community of Christ must render, we can *only* serve God and never the worldly powers as well.

In its binding to the Word of God *alone,* the church makes no power claims over against others, as the accusation of intolerance claims. The error of that accusation is that in its polemic against such a danger, it represses the decisive thing. It is true that the church has no claims to make. But the one Word of God makes its own claim, and indeed first of all upon the church. To be sure, that accusation quite properly speaks out against power claims made *by the church,* but it does this in such a way that it appears to direct itself against the unconditional right of the *Lord* of the church to his church. What excludes churchly claims to power is not some kind of general relativism but the legitimate claim of God to his church. The one Word of God raises this claim to his church. When the church evades that claim, then it profoundly obscures the fact that it is the church *of Jesus Christ.* God's Word makes *the* claim upon it that we, the Christians, must hear this Word, that we have to "trust and obey" it "in life and in death." His Word makes this claim upon the church by simultaneously rejecting the seductive assumption that "the church could and would have to acknowledge as a source of *its* proclamation, apart from and besides this one Word of God, still other events and powers, figures and truths, as God's revelation." A church that withdraws from this claim and this rejection violates the first commandment. To assert then that its violation of the first commandment is a justified concern doubles the damage.

4. Christians and Jews

Let us return to Pinchas Lapide's criticism that the first Barmen thesis could become "indirectly the sponsor of a social anti-Semitism."[24] It is correct and profoundly fateful that the Barmen Declaration, particularly in its first thesis, does not imply in any way that it stands and must stand in an essential bond with the Jews. However this omission is explained, the thesis is thereby lacking in the precision and clarity that would have given it the force of an obligation in the time that immediately followed. But one should not overlook the fact that the anti-Semitism of that time was not argued Christologically but in terms of the *Volk*, that is, ethnically, which is why baptized Jews were also ostracized and persecuted. Further, the fact that the so-called "Confessing Church" would later remain silent over against the persecution of the Jews was not due to its faithfulness to the Barmen Declaration. For the most part, it preferred also not to be reminded of the Barmen Declaration in the times that followed. It is more important to understand that it is certainly wrong to assert that the Barmen Declaration took no stance on the anti-Jewish tactics going on then because its thought was itself anti-Jewish.

To understand that, we have to broaden our investigation. Hitler's revolutionary method was his desire *first* to get the media under control. Thus, his henchmen went *first* after the opposing voices, some of which were certainly Jewish, convinced that once such voices were silenced the population could be led wherever the regime wanted. The fact is that such critics were the first to be put into concentration camps. Conversely, the Evangelical Church was, in the eyes of the state, not a serious opponent. In this context one needs to hear the thesis that Karl Barth published a few weeks before the Barmen Synod, titled "Church Opposition in 1933." It is a kind of anticipatory commentary on the first Barmen thesis, and I quote from it: "The protest against the heresy of the German Christians cannot begin with the Aryan Laws, the repudiation of the Old Testament, the Arianism of German-Christian Christology, the naturalism and Pelagianism of the German-

24. Cf. note 4.

Christian doctrine of justification and sanctification, the state's divinization of the German-Christian ethic. The protest must fundamentally be directed against the fact (which is the *source* of all the individual heresies) that the German Christians assert that, *next* to Holy Scripture as the sole source of revelation, the German nation (Volk), its history and its contemporary politics, constitute a second source of revelation, thus revealing that they believe in 'another God'."[25] The point is not that the law against non-Aryans was not to be regarded as all that important. That would mean that the church would also have to downplay the very grave errors regarding the Old Testament, Christology, doctrines of justification and sanctification, and the idolization of the state. To do that would mean that the church would completely cease to be *church* at all. Barth's statement is directed expressly against the *roots* of the "corruption of the *entire* Evangelical Church," which had been spreading for a long time already. That corruption was based on the view that a second source of revelation should be placed at the side of the one source of revelation. Precisely at that point, a belief in "another," a *false* God is introduced. This always makes the church helpless over against her own corruption.

It becomes clear now that by the elimination of the roots of its corruption, the church is transferred into a new situation. If the conjunction, the "and" between the one and the allegedly second source of revelation is removed, then the church will regain its identity and demonstrate what it really is. Then its first concern will not be how it can *conform* itself; rather, its concern will be that to which it must in all faithfulness *confess*. Then the confessors will no longer view themselves merely as *one* party within the church, in which they view the German Christians as another party *in* the church. They *themselves* would then become the church, the church from which the German Christians had in truth departed. Then they remove the error on their *own* side as though they could politically advocate National Socialism, and yet be a church that was pure and untouched by it. Then they become in fact the "churchly opposition," free to confess over against the powers and

---

25. K. Barth, "Kirchliche Opposition 1933," in K. Barth, *Lutherfeier, Theologische Existenz heute* 4 (München: Chr. Kaiser Verlag, 1933), p. 20.

principalities of the age. This then becomes *especially* important in regard to the points mentioned before, the position on the Old Testament and the position on the Jews. Why? Because this now excludes formulating their position on these issues using that second source of revelation. The church will obviously rebut what is claimed about the relation to the Jews based on that second source with what is to be heard from the only true source of revelation, that is, the biblical source. Then, the exclusive character of the statement that there is *one* Word will be understandable to Jews as the acknowledgment of the exclusivity of the first commandment: "You shall have *no other* gods before me." Then Christians will understand their saying that Jesus Christ is the one Word not as a wall of separation but as a bridge built by God in their relationship with the Jews. They will do so because God has committed himself never to be another than the One he has demonstrated and revealed himself to be in Christ, as the *Reconciler.* A very long time ago, that critic of Christendom, Friedrich Nietzsche, had understood better than most Christians that they abandon *themselves* when they abandon the Jews; he declared: "Christianity is to be understood solely from the ground out of which it grew . . . ; 'Salvation comes from the Jews.'"[26]

Am I inserting something wrong into the thesis with this interpretation? I don't think so, because at least a majority of the Barmen delegates knew the sermon that Barth had published in December 1933, and which he also sent to Hitler, as documentation of "an authentic representation of what the Evangelical Church is and should be." In his conclusion Barth makes its real point: "that in faith in Christ who was himself a Jew . . . one simply *cannot participate* in the disdain and abuse of the Jews which is the political agenda of the day"; it is a "regression into the purest paganism."[27] In the sermon itself, four basic thoughts are developed, based upon Romans 15:5-13. (1) "Jesus Christ was a Jew." The Son of God assumed this people's nature and blood, and did so in such a way that we who come from other ethnicities stand, in distinc-

---

26. F. Nietzsche, *Der Antichrist: Fluch auf das Christentum,* Nr. 24, ET: F. Nietzsche, *The Antichrist,* ed. H. L. Mencken (New York: A. Knopf, 1920), no. 74, p. 78.

27. E. Busch, *Unter dem Bogen des einen Bundes: Karl Barth und die Juden* (Neukirchen-Vluyn: Neukirchener Verlag, 1996), p. 173.

tion from this people, before a locked door. (2) The advantage of the Jews consists in the fact that it was God's pleasure to elect them and to conclude a covenant with them, out of free grace and not because of the goodness of their character. Whoever turns against the Jews also turns against the God of free grace. (3) John 4:22: "Salvation is from the Jews." They themselves open that locked door in that they treat Christ in the very same way in which all other peoples would have treated him. Precisely because God does not reject them for that, God's goodness is now valid for them as it is for us sinners who are heathens. And (4), this leads to the inexorable command, "Accept one another." For, as he formulates it in the climax of the sermon, Jesus "sees us as Jews struggling with the true God" — the literal meaning of the word *Israel!* — and he sees us as *goyim,* as "heathens at peace with the false gods, but he sees us both as 'children of the living God.'"[28] Here the biblical-theological and thus the humane view of the relationship with the Jews counters the false, biological, and thus inhumane way of seeing it.

One final comment: In the confessional collections of many churches we find today next to each other the Barmen Declaration and theses about the solidarity of Christians and Jews. Have the people in these churches given any thought to the way in which both fit with each other? They are not to be understood as a mutual contradiction, and the only way to avoid doing that is to make this double emphasis clear: Christians' solidarity with Jews does not happen by evading Jesus Christ, but only *in* Jesus Christ. And, we have not yet rightly understood Jesus Christ as the one Word of God if we Christians have him in some other way than in his solidarity with the Jews, which is thus *our* solidarity. Thus we say that Christians are not God's chosen people in place of the Jews, but rather that they, the Jews, are elect, and we are, thank God, called into them. This we believe (with Rom. 15:8) in that we believe the reconciliation of Jesus Christ as the confirmation of the promises that God has given to the mothers and the fathers of his people. In this way the Word, which was in the *beginning,* is that Word which according to 1 Peter 1:25 "endures forever."

28. K. Barth, "Predigt über Römer 15,5-13," in K. Barth, *Die Kirche Jesu Christi, Theologische Existenz heute* 5 (München: Chr. Kaiser Verlag, 1933), pp. 13-18.

The Rigorous Gospel and the Gracious Law

"Christ Jesus, whom God made our wisdom, our righteousness and sanctification and redemption" (1 Cor. 1:30).

As Jesus Christ is God's assurance of the forgiveness of all our sins, so in the same way and with the same seriousness is he also God's mighty claim upon our whole life. Through him befalls us a joyful deliverance from the godless fetters of this world for a free, grateful service to his creatures.

We reject the false doctrine, as though there were areas of our life in which we would not belong to Jesus Christ, but to other lords — areas in which we would not need justification and sanctification through him.

The philosopher Immanuel Kant stated: "Enlightenment is man's release from his self-incurred tutelage. . . . 'Have courage to use your own reason!' — that is the motto of enlightenment."[1] It is a good thing for Christians to take this to heart and, above all, to understand it in the right way. For these propositions do not contest the fact that ethics deals with obedience in relation to God's command. They contest against an ethics of slavish and blind obedience and for an ethics of "free obedience," as Calvin had already put it.[2] One may understand

---

1. I. Kant, *Beantwortung der Frage: Was ist Aufklärung?*, in *Kants Werke* (Darmstadt: Wissenschaftliche Buchgesellschaft, 1964), vol. 9, p. 53; ET: "What Is Enlightenment?," Immanuel Kant, *Philosophical Writings*, ed. E. Behler (New York: Continuum, 1991), p. 263.

2. J. Calvin, *Institutio christianae religionis*, II.8.15; ET: Calvin, *Institutes of the Christian*

the second Barmen thesis, which is now our theme, as a foundation for Christian ethics. "Christian" does not mean in this context that we are dealing with a special, religious morality. "Christian" means here that ethics stands within the framework of liberation from wrong bonds. Therefore, such an ethics cannot speak about law and its claim before it has addressed the *gospel* and God's *assurance*. And it cannot speak of those without immediately and consequently dealing with God's *law,* his *claim.* By speaking about all of this in such a framework, it addresses Christian ethics in a foundational way.

1. The Connection of Gospel and Law

Let us recapture the situation in which the content of the second thesis was first uttered. The thesis is directed not against Luther and Calvin's doctrine of the two kingdoms. *That* doctrine rejected the idea that the state could prescribe to the church what should be preached in it, and on the other hand, it rejected the idea that the church, forgetting its own task, could conduct itself like a state ruler. The Barmen thesis, however, is directed against a modern version of the two kingdoms doctrine in Christian ethics, in particular, against a doctrine of the "autonomies" as it was formulated by Max Weber around 1900.[3] According to this doctrine, all the worldly areas of life bear their own legitimacy within themselves in such a way that one can and may not intervene in their processes with a command of the biblical God. As a consequence, either there is no divine command at all or one must identify the worldly autonomies with the law of God. Whichever the option, Christian ethics then merely provides a good conscience for smooth compliance with the worldly autonomies and perhaps, in addition to that, a few rules for moral respectability for one's private life. In 1933, this view dominated and was then intensively focused upon the following doctrine: The church's task in its own sphere was

---

Religion, trans. F. L. Battles, Library of Christian Classics (Philadelphia: Westminster, 1960), II.viii.15, 1:380-81.

3. M. Weber, *Gesammelte Aufsätze zur Religionssoziologie,* I (1920), p. 552.

to proclaim *only* the gospel, without instructions for daily life in the "world." The law that one is to obey in the "world" is encountered by Christians *solely* in the worldly orders of the state. And since the law is not connected with the gospel, the law comes more clearly to the fore as the legal powers of the world function in more authoritarian and merciless ways. For this reason, the church could welcome the nationalist-racist state and say, "By submitting myself to the law of *this* state, I am being obedient to *God* and heaping no guilt upon myself. If something evil happens, then the obedient subjects will not be guilty, but solely the state power, if at all." This view of the law signifies the de-Christianization of God's law by means of Christian theology. This is where the second Barmen thesis carries out a radical course correction. We shall examine in greater detail how it does that.

As we heard before, Thesis One speaks of Jesus as the *"one* Word of God." It also says that the proper *hearing* of this Word takes place in two actions: trusting and obeying. What corresponds to the one Word is one thing alone, our faith. But this one faith includes three dimensions: hearing, trusting, and obeying. Where *this* Word is concerned, hearing the Word that became human in Jesus Christ cannot be superficial. In the act of hearing, the message comes to us in such a way that there is no option other than to place our entire trust in the one Word of God. This leads unavoidably to the linking of our trust with obedience, and prepares the way for what Thesis Two develops. The one Word has two forms: *assurance* of the forgiveness of all our sins and *claim* upon our entire life — gospel and law, God's gift of grace and God's command, our justification and our sanctification. Because the Word of God is such assurance, we may place all our trust in it. And because the Word of God is such a claim, we must obey it with all our lives. Gospel and law must be differentiated. But both are forms of the same one Word of God and thus are not to be separated or seen as opposite to each other. If one speaks first of the law and only then of the gospel, one ends up in a dual difficulty. The law will be understood as an opposite to the gospel from which the gospel liberates us, *and* we will not be able to differentiate between what God commands and what earthly powers require. In Thesis Two the Barmen Declaration carries out an inversion of the two concepts in the sequence "gospel and law." Accordingly, we speak now *first* of God's assurance, of his *gospel,* but do so under the theme, "the rigorous gospel."

2. The Rigorous Gospel

We could also use Bonhoeffer's formulation and speak of "costly grace," as in his book *The Cost of Discipleship*.[4] I will present the argument in three thoughts.

(1) The second thesis begins with the citation of 1 Corinthians 1:30: "Christ Jesus, whom God made our wisdom, our righteousness and sanctification and redemption." According to the thesis, this biblical statement makes clear at the outset that the assurance, the gospel, is not something that satisfies all human wishes, not something whose goodness one can calculate without God, and then require of God as a product that God is to produce or that one could get from somewhere else. The gospel is rigorous in the particular sense that what it is and effects is rigorously defined according to the witness of Holy Scripture. Whatever in life otherwise benefits the human person may indeed be for her a parable of the gospel. But the human is thereby often grasping after something that only appears to benefit her, and she often flees from that which is really good for her. Here it is necessary to inquire after the witness of Scripture. From it the *gospel* is to be heard as the epitome of that which benefits the human person.

The thesis that follows this biblical citation is a direct exegesis of that biblical word. According to this exegesis, the biblical statement is to be understood in the following way. The word "wisdom" connects to the earlier verses in 1 Corinthians in which Paul speaks of the wisdom of God that appears to be foolishness to the world and yet is superior to the wisdom of the world. In our verse, we are told what that wisdom, into which Christ is made for us, consists of for those who are Christians. Three concepts are given for it: righteousness, sanctification, and redemption. In the Barmen thesis the first two concepts are taken up

---

4. D. Bonhoeffer, *Nachfolge* (Berlin, 1954), ch. 1, pp. 11ff.; ET: *The Cost of Discipleship*, trans. R. H. Fuller and J. Booth (New York: Macmillan, 1964), ch. 1.

and translated into assurance and claim, or justification and sanctification. And what of the concept "redemption"? It occurs then in the second part of the affirmative thesis in the translated form "joyful deliverance," and is used there as a term that brackets justification and sanctification together as two sides of the liberation effected through Christ. It is, on the one hand, liberation *from* the godless fetters and on the other hand liberation *for* free and grateful service. We note how in listening *rigorously* to the witness of Holy Scripture this begins to work in its hearers, and we note how the understanding of gospel and law and the understanding of their relationship to each other become clear when we recognize, under the guidance of the scriptural text, that *Jesus Christ* is the subject of the entire process.

(2) God's gospel is *rigorous* and his grace *costly* because it is the "forgiveness of all our sins" out of God's grace alone. The concepts "forgiveness" and "justification" are parallel in Thesis Two, and they can only be so if forgiveness is not understood as a careless wiping away of sins, or as a merely verbal excusing. Such an excusing would not take sin seriously and would ultimately not be the forgiving of *all* sins. For then we would suddenly come upon sins that were so grave that one could only conclude that there could *not* be any forgiveness for them! The true forgiveness of sins never takes place in such a way that even the smallest of sins is forgotten and treated lightly. In the true forgiveness of sins we will finally grasp what we would have earlier contested, namely, how very much we have not deservèd it at all. But in the true forgiveness of sins it is not *as if* our sins were only apparently forgiven. In it, they *are* in fact forgiven us — not forgotten, but relegated to our past.

It was necessary to emphasize this at that time. In many of the confessional texts set out in the church in 1933, the idea of a divinely intended special character of or preference for the German person and nation, in contrast with other people and nations, played a role that permeated all of Christian doctrine. This was directly contradicted by the statement that *all* people are equally sinners and are in need of the forgiveness of *all* sins. Thus we should note that even if, in the thesis, forgiveness or justification is so tightly connected with sanctification, it is still very clear that forgiveness is not ascribed to a person because of the service one does for God's creatures as one who is sanctified.

There is nothing the human can contribute to this, not even a contribution that might be derived from God's grace. The gracious assurance of forgiveness *alone* is what frees us from our sins. Note, too, the language about *all* our sins. This is a prelude to what is then expressed in the second half of the statement: forgiveness takes place after the model of Israel's exodus from Egypt, in which there is the joyous deliverance not only of some individuals but rather of a community from the godless fetters of the world. There is liberation from a system of injustice, lying, and violence that enslaves the entire community.

(3) The gospel is rigorous and grace is costly also because there is in it a deliverance from *sin* through the forgiveness of all sins, but no release from *Jesus Christ* as the one Word of God. The freedom that he gives us is freedom in commitment to and responsibility before him. If forgiveness were to lead to a departure from Christ — as, for example, after recovering from an illness one no longer needs the doctor — then in *this* instance the human would have fallen back into the world of sin. Sin lies behind us to the extent that Christ is *not* behind us but rather with us, and we with him. Grace becomes cheap grace to the extent that one makes use of it on occasion only to give the old Adam breathing space to return with a good conscience to the old life under the dominion of corrupt powers, back to the godless fetters of this world. Such a division of life into two parts, one in which one worships God in the church, and the other worldly part in which one follows the slogans of national-racist unity under the one Führer, is a system where in fact such a relapse into the godless fetters of the world is reinterpreted as a matter of tolerable normality. Matters are not improved when theologians such as Emanuel Hirsch and Gerhard Kittel attempt to explain to the victims of unjust state action that its harshness is tolerable, rather than condemning it.[5] Where the church does not believe and confess God as the one Lord over the different spheres of church and state, there the church is capable of the impossible: there the church wants to serve God *and* Hitler, and thus it will serve *only* Hitler. It is certainly true that, in spite of forgiveness, we constantly experience backsliding.

---

5. E. Busch, *Karl Barth und die Juden* (Neukirchen-Vluyn: Neukirchener Verlag, 1996), p. 102.

But there is no explanation for this. Christ has forgiven us our sins for the very reason that we might no longer be subject to those sins but belong to him. That is the theme of the rejection statement that is directed against the false doctrine "as though there were areas of our life in which we would not belong to Jesus Christ, but to other lords — areas in which we would not need justification and sanctification through him." This view is described as a heresy, as a lie. The lie is overcome solely by the truth. And this is the truth, that there are no areas of life "in which we do not belong to Jesus Christ," as the thesis states in the language of the Heidelberg Catechism.[6]

Having considered the theme of the "rigor" of the gospel, we now turn to the theme of the *law* of God, again from three perspectives. In order to signal the relationship of his law with the gospel, we shall speak of God's *gracious* law.

3. God's Gracious Law

I shall discuss this theme in three steps.

(1) If Jesus Christ is God's assurance and "with the same seriousness" also God's *claim,* and if we are not actually hearing God's word when it is only assurance for us and not claim as well, then hearing and attending to *God's command* is inseparable from the church's most essential task, which is the proclamation of the gospel. For then he not only pardons us, but he governs us too. The church would be unfaithful to its most essential task if, in accordance with God's command, it did not endeavor to ground and develop an evangelical ethic. It would not take the forgiveness of sins seriously if it did not take the question of the action God commands of us with the same seriousness. The unity of the one Word of God would be put into question if God's assurance were uncoupled from his claim to our life. The inseparability of the divine command from the divine gift of grace means negatively that no inner-worldly law is identical with the divine command, as was

6. Heidelberg Catechism, q. 1, Presbyterian Church (U.S.A.), *Book of Confessions* (Louisville: Office of the General Assembly, 1999).

asserted in 1933 virtually everywhere in the church. The German Christians expressed it in December 1933 very crudely when they said that God's "law speaks to us out of the history of our folk that has grown out of our blood and soil."[7] No, "we must obey God rather than any human authority" — this statement in Acts 5:29 is always valid and not just when a conflict arises. It is the fundamental principle of evangelical ethics. One does not ask, in such an ethics, where there is space somewhere in the midst of human laws for a divine command. Conversely, one does ask, in such an ethics, how human laws can be held accountable before the divine command. Human laws are, for Christians, not as such already divine command; they are rather the place from which one neither can nor normally should escape, but where one tests whether and to what extent and in which sense they are to be followed or not, in obedience to God, or whether resistance is called for.

What is then God's command? In this thesis, the exciting novelty is that the basis of evangelical ethics is not a program, not a principle, not a categorical imperative, but rather a person, Jesus Christ. As God's assurance, he is "also God's mighty claim upon our whole life." He is the foundation of evangelical ethics: God has sent him into the world as the demonstration of his love. In him God has made himself responsible for his creatures. He has bought human beings at great cost (1 Cor. 6:20) so that they might not be the slaves of other humans but the children of God. God lays no claim upon humanity before he first lays claim upon himself for them, thus fulfilling his will and his command for their benefit. It is not as an empty claim but as an already-fulfilled command that we are confronted by "God's mighty claim upon our whole life." Thus, there is no requirement laid upon us to fulfill God's command first of all. God claims us so that we might *attach ourselves* to God's command already fulfilled in Christ. And we obey him by our demonstration that we belong to him.

Basically, evangelical ethics is instruction for following Jesus Christ, for discipleship. Thus there are two aspects to evangelical ethics. First, in that Jesus Christ precedes and leads us as his disciples, his

---

7. A. Burgsmüller and R. Weth, eds., *Die Barmer Theologische Erklärung* (Neukirchen-Vluyn: Neukirchener Verlag, 1983), p. 34.

person is the warrant for us that following him will always happen along certain basic lines. We will mention a few of these. In this action, things will always serve people rather than people serving things. In it people are free in *fellowship* and in fellowship are *free*. In it love will be carried out in *truth*, and the truth in *love*. In the discipleship of Jesus Christ the goodness of the shared life will be measured by the extent to which the least ones are helped to receive their rights. In his discipleship we ask again and again how all life is to be protected and preserved as far as possible. In his discipleship we do not act in the anxiety and worry that we might be forsaken by God but rather in the joy at his presence. These perspectives disclose the basic lines along which Christian action will take place. But this is not to stipulate principles. Rather, and this is the second aspect of an evangelical ethics, what it means practically to act along these lines in the particular and actual challenges will always be an open question. This question should be answered in always new concrete decisions. Discipleship does not mean insistently taking a position and staying there. Discipleship means *moving* along a path. On this path we come across surprising new situations, sometimes from one day to the next. Yesterday's solutions do not help us then. In the light of Jesus Christ we are to ask anew from situation to situation: What is commanded of us *now* in *this* setting? How will life be protected here and peace served and the truth honored? To do this requires expertise, thought, wisdom, and courage, the reading of the Bible and of secular sources of information.

(2) If Jesus Christ is both God's assurance and with the same seriousness God's mighty claim upon our entire life, then a further important decision has thus been made. It has to do with the understanding of the *character* of God's command. Based on the interconnectedness of God's assurance and claim, God's command is not in opposition to God's grace. Therefore it cannot be hollowed out so that it is no more than the mere form of a command, regardless of whom or what it commands, as has been taught in modern theology. Thus one can see that it is not hard, repressive, merciless coercion, but has the character of good, yes, gracious guidance. It only becomes graceless if we want to hear the law divorced from God's grace. To understand that, we must gain clarity about the relationship between God's assurance and claim.

God's assurance is our exoneration from "*all* our sins." All our backsliding does not change what is now utterly true: God will *never let go* of those whom he declares and makes free of sin. He releases them *from* their sin, but he does not release them *into* a further life in sin. The fact that he does not let go of them means that they now belong to him. And that they now belong to him means that he lays a legitimate claim upon their entire life. That is how God's assurance and claim are related to each other.

In his claim upon us, God does not take back with one hand what he earlier gave with the other, his assurance. This is how he demonstrates that his acquittal *from* our sins and his acquittal *to* our life in fellowship with him go hand in hand. Thus he gives us guidance about how to continue in the freedom to which he has freed us in Christ (Gal. 5:1). He does not require of us the begrudging fulfillment of obligation but rather he expects of us our gratitude for the beneficence we have received. The one who calls the weary and heavy-laden to himself does indeed say, "take my yoke upon you," but this yoke is easy and his burden is light (Matt. 11:29f.) — in contrast to everything that otherwise is wearisome and burdensome for us. This is how the introduction to the Decalogue interprets the way the Ten Commandments are to be understood, as Calvin said: "[God's people] have been freed from miserable bondage that they may, in obedience and readiness to serve, worship him as the author of their freedom."[8] The second Barmen thesis puts it in a corresponding way by explaining the relationship between God's assurance and claim in Jesus Christ thus: "Through him befalls us a joyful deliverance from the godless fetters of this world for a free, grateful service to his creatures." What the theologians in 1933 called obligatory divine "law" is here brusquely defined as "godless fetters" from which God frees us. And if the God who frees us also lays claim upon us, then it is clear that we can only follow his command gladly, freely, and thankfully. It is always a misunderstood and misused law of God whenever it is repulsive to us.

The freedom into which God's assurance relocates us and that we under God's claim are to prove in practice is not arbitrary. If man on

---

8. J. Calvin, *Institutio christianae religionis,* II.8.15; ET: *Institutes,* II.viii.15, 1:380.

his own rebels against godless fetters, then he tends to fall back into a godless lack of commitments. That has as little to do with real freedom as does that godless bondage. We have the freedom into which God's assurance places us only and always in God's connection with us. Accordingly, we can have the freedom that we are to practice under God's claim only in our connection with God and with all those with whom he connects himself; for they are made in this process into our "neighbors." We can persist in the freedom for which Christ has made us free only as long as we live according to the double command of love, in connection with God and with our neighbors. According to Paul, our calling to freedom proves itself solely in this imperative: "through love become slaves to one another" (Gal. 5:13). In the words of the second Barmen thesis, our liberation through Christ *out* of the godless fetters is our liberation "*for* a free, grateful service to his creatures." In this service, we encounter many whom we would rather not love, because they are disagreeable to us, enemies not friends. But let us not look at them in terms of what they mean to *us!* Let us look at them in terms of what they mean to *God!* They are *his* creatures! And if we see them in that way, then as a matter of principle, our service of love cannot be denied to anyone. In such love, we can and we must do all kinds of things: stand together with others, support and even put up with others, but also perhaps contradict and oppose others firmly. Whether or not we are doing this rightly is determined by the fact that in everything that happens, even when we have to say "no" to their activities, we are still basically saying "yes" to them and thus *loving* them, and all the while doing so unobtrusively, but decisively.

(3) If God does not let go in Christ of those whom he releases in Christ from their wrongness, then this has the aforementioned significance. Then God's claim on us does not merely mean that God commands us to do this or that. Rather, in whatever he commands us to do, he claims us as those who *belong* to him. Whatever we do, we are his children. And whatever we must do, we should do it as the responsibility of those who belong to him as the members of his family. The focusing point of this insight is that we no longer can, so to speak, move from the church's space into so-called "life out there" as though we were going into a totally different world, a world in which what counts

is very different and in which we would exist as something other than his people. What we encounter there is not the law of *God*. That would mean that we were entering into another dominion that would conceal or even abrogate the truth that Christ is our Lord and brother, the one who had already spoken to us in the assurance of the gospel. Instead, we enter there as those who are already addressed by God's command. We enter there as those who are already claimed by him and bound to him. Out there we will encounter no law that can abolish this.

This does not contest that there are diverse areas of our lives. We are not in the church everywhere. There is the area of work, of economics, of culture and information, the area of science and politics. In every area there are particular factors to pay attention to and to think about. In every area there is a distinctive logic and way of functioning that requires precise knowledge and sensitive orientation if one wants to be part of the action and discourse. What we vehemently contest is the idea that the diversity of areas and the requirement of competence in order to move and speak in them should mean that we are released from belonging to Christ and freed from acting as his disciples. While in the diverse areas this may all happen in differing ways, we are everywhere never anything other than members of his people, and as such we are responsible to him. This presupposes that Jesus Christ bears responsibility for all areas of life. He contradicts the thesis of the autonomies of the diverse areas of life. Were that true, these areas would be automats that function independently according to their own immanent laws, without any intervention from outside. All of them would be forsaken by God and his good Spirit. That is not true of them. For that reason, when we enter into these areas, we are not entering territory that of necessity would have to be totally alien to us as Christians. And thus we are not doing something wrong when we act there as those who belong to Jesus Christ and not to other masters, or to ourselves.

Let us look more closely at the phrase that God's claim relates to "our *whole* life." This phrase does away with the notion that life is to be divided into two spheres, an inner and outer one, a spiritual and a worldly, a psychic and a material. Where people think and act according to the pattern of such a division, it is unavoidable that, even when comfortably "with my Lord Jesus" in the first sphere, in the second, one is always subject to other masters. This results in an introverted church that retreats to concentrate on the sacral care of souls, and looks upon the material and the bodily as of less value, perhaps even holding them in contempt and consigning their organization to others. For that sort of church what happens in the world is openly or secretly irrelevant. It considers itself to be above emulating the Good Samaritan, getting involved with the downtrodden and victimized. Its salt has lost its savor and has become unusable (Matt. 5:13). If God's claim encompasses "our *whole* life," then this comfortable division must be a thing of the past. Then Christianity will and must act in accordance with the fine saying of the sage Paracelsus, "Whoever comforts the soul of his fellow man should also comfort his body."[9] It will then delight at the wonder that what must be done anyway is done very well, and what makes sense anyway is done sensibly.

Christian ethics is an ethic of freedom. To say it again, it has to do with a freedom that has as little to do with coercion as it has to do with arbitrariness. It is a freedom that is not practiced in isolation but rather in connectedness with God and his children who are "my" brothers and sisters. But still, in this sense, it is an ethic of freedom. There may be situations in which one swims against the current and still cooperates with others. In so doing, one might be able to arrive at good agreements with one's non-Christian fellows. In this freedom one will occasionally have to demolish some things critically, but only in order to preserve things worth holding onto or to risk new things. Behind all these endeavors there will be *prayer* — and it will become quite obvious whether *that* is really what is behind it all. According to the prayer of Jesus, the Lord's Prayer, our prayer engages first of all the world's rebellion against God and asks that his name should be hallowed, that his will should be done, and that his kingdom should come. It then asks for God's engagement in human distress, that he should take to heart humanity's hunger and thirst, its failure and guilt, its oppression by evil powers. Such praying is not merely preparation for the ethical conduct of Christians. It is its first act.

9. See H. Urner, "Paracelsus als Christ," in *Evangelische Theologie* (1948-49), p. 300.

47

The One Lord in the Fellowship
of Brothers and Sisters

"Rather, speaking the truth in love, we are to grow up in every way into him who is the head, into Christ, from whom the whole body [is] joined and knit together" (Eph. 4:15-16).

The Christian Church is the congregation of the brethren in which Jesus Christ acts presently as the Lord in Word and Sacrament through the Holy Spirit. As the church of pardoned sinners, it has to testify in the midst of a sinful world, with its faith as with its obedience, with its message as with its order, that it is solely his property, and it lives and wants to live solely from his comfort and from his direction in the expectation of his appearance.

We reject the false doctrine, as though the church were permitted to abandon the form of its message and order to its own pleasure or to changes in prevailing ideological and political convictions.

In 1557 John Calvin wrote a letter to women in Paris who were imprisoned on account of their faith, in which he said: "But since it has pleased God to call you as well as men . . . , you must not [be cowardly]. Since we have a common salvation in Him, it is necessary that all with one accord, men as well as women, should maintain His cause."[1] Calvin speaks of an in-

---

1. *J. Calvins Lebenswerk in seinen Briefen,* trans. R. Schwarz (Neukirchen-Vluyn: Neukirchener Verlag, 1962), p. 916; ET: J. Bonnet, *Letters of John Calvin,* vol. 3 (New York: B. Franklin, 1972), pp. 364-65.

sight that we must constantly discover anew: Where humans are called together by their one good shepherd, they are also related to one another as a community in which every person lives as an important member of a working fellowship. In 1934 this knowledge was obscured, and in the Barmen Declaration it was rediscovered. The third Barmen thesis deals with this. On the one hand, this thesis is the *consequence* that follows upon the two preceding theses. It is, on the other hand, the practical *center* of the confession. It has become common usage to speak of the theological controversy in the Protestant churches during the Nazi period as the "church struggle," the *Kirchenkampf.* That does not imply that the church at the time was united in its fight against some enemy attacking it from outside. That was, to begin with, totally impossible because the church was not "united" at all. But beyond that, it was impossible because the church did not for the most part see the totalitarian state as an enemy of any kind, but instead saw it as very welcome. What the affirmative position on the current events taken by representatives of the church really demonstrated was that the church did not seriously know any longer what it really means to be *church,* to be the church *of Jesus Christ,* which belongs to him and is ruled by him. To be sure, they *thought* they knew what it meant. But the *judgment* of the third Barmen thesis was that the church had, in truth, become spineless, and that it had to struggle and then write down in the form of a confession what it had struggled for: we are the church of Jesus Christ. What is confessed in the third thesis, including its explanation in Thesis Four, is in a concise but highly crafted concentration a complete doctrine of the church. This should now be explored in four thematic steps. Thesis Four then takes a fifth step, which will be considered in its own section.

1. The Biblical Clarification

The main statement of the positive thesis about what the Christian church, the church of Jesus Christ, means, can be summarized in this formula: it is a Christocracy of brothers and sisters.[2] Thesis Three states,

---

2. See Karl Barth, *KD* IV/2, pp. 770f. = *CD* IV/2, pp. 680-81.

"The Christian Church is the congregation of brothers and sisters in which Jesus Christ acts presently as the Lord. . . ." This thesis arises anew out of the hearing of Holy Scripture, initially of two passages that the thesis does not directly cite but certainly alludes to. The church is understood, first, along the lines of the pericope about the true family of Jesus in Mark 3:33-34: "And looking at those who sat around him, he said, 'Here are my mother and my brothers.'" For, "'Whoever does the will of God is my brother, and sister, and mother.'" That is the Christian church, the community assembled around Christ, he in their midst and they around him, surrounding him. They have not joined themselves together on account of their common interest. He has called them together, and they have followed his call. He makes himself present to them as the Living One among them, and because of that they are situated in his presence. Here the second biblical passage alluded to intervenes: Matthew 23:8, 10: "For you have *one* teacher [Christ] and you are all *brothers.*" That is the Christian church. "Doing the will of God," as was just cited, means that those who are gathered around him are already *doing* God's will. They are doing it by being gathered around him, listening to him, looking at him, being focused upon him in soul and body, letting him set them aright and show them the way.

Thesis Three begins *expressly* with the citation of the extraordinarily dense passage, Ephesians 4:15-16: "Rather, speaking the truth in love, we are to grow up in every way into him who is the head, into Christ, from whom the whole body [is] joined and knit together." The relationship between Christ and his congregation is understood here in terms of the relation between head and body: the head is over the body and rules over it and is at the same time seamlessly connected to it. This head of the body is the only *one*, next to which there is none other, no subheads. All the others are *members* of the body. The entire body is characterized by the fact that it is the ensemble of *diverse* members with different functions, in order thus to be *one* body, the body of its one head. The instructive thing about Ephesians 4 is that the discourse here treats of a double movement, a movement of the body in relation to the head, and one of the head in relation to the body. From the head the entire body is *joined together;* the various members are knit together so that they form a unity. Out of the various members Christ makes

51

one congregation, in which everyone has a task. This all precedes the action of the congregation's members, precedes it in that Christ calls them to their appropriate action. And their action then takes place in two directions: in the direction of the *love* that confirms the mutual connectedness of all the congregation's members, and in the direction of the *growth* in their shared connectedness with the one who is the head of the congregation.

2. Threatened Church

The third thesis appeals to Scripture in a concrete situation. The challenge is that the church finds and receives support and orientation in a threat that must *be removed,* must be *rejected,* so that the church can be the *church.* It sees itself here as profoundly threatened — seriously and decisively threatened not from outside, not from the world around it, not even from the Nazi regime. The *real,* the life-threatening jeopardy of the church does not come from outside. It generally comes from a place where the church as a rule least expects it — that is, from *itself,* through a "false doctrine" that has gradually gained general acknowledgment and validation and begun to penetrate and define its practice, without opposition. It was so very threatened by this in 1934 that Thesis Three, when it speaks of a church of *sinners* in the midst of a world of sin, must be understood as emphatically *concrete.* It was going to be difficult to concede that a position held in the church, perhaps advocated with conviction and finding broad acceptance, was a "*false* doctrine." But the Word of God as it confronts the church in the form of a biblical passage can open its eyes. That is why such listening to God's Word belongs to the church's confession and does not merely precede its confessing. What this Word, having been heard, meant for the threatened church must be expressly stated. But it must be said within the context of the scriptural Word that was heard first.

The church puts *itself* in jeopardy — either in its *retreat* from the world into an interior space to attend to a sacral activity that is an end in itself, or in its *conforming* to the world around it, to which it surrenders. The church is threatened when it contests Jesus' statement, "You are the salt of the earth" (Matt. 5:13), either by letting its savory message remain unused or by diluting it. According to the statement of rejection in Thesis Three this twofold danger is basically one and the same. Whether one withdraws from the world with one's biblical message, as the centrist party of the church had wanted to do since July 1933, or one wants to extend the world's activity to include the message of the church as the German Christians did — either way, they allowed a very problematic process to move ahead unproblematically. They concurred, even if now and again there was some talk about the need for theological courage. This is the danger to which the church subjects itself with the "false doctrine, as though the church were permitted to abandon the *form* [!] of its message and order to its own pleasure or to changes in prevailing ideological and political convictions." When the church, as was generally acknowledged at that time, conforms its *order* to the reigning convictions, then what follows will be in line with the poet Schiller's statement: "If the purple cloak falls, the duke must [fall] after it,"[3] which means, the church will also conform its *message* or its form to those convictions. This doctrine was already widespread in the Protestant Church before the Nazi period. According to the legal scholar Rudolf Sohm (at the end of the nineteenth century), the true church of Christ is invisible and as such "free from any legal structure."[4] The legal shape of the visible church, therefore, is for him a purely worldly matter. That persuaded many, far too many. The theologian Emanuel Hirsch declared without hesitation, "The church's constitution must be conformed to the state."[5]

It was by no means only the German Christians who applied this doctrine to the situation in the Third Reich. The opinion was widely held that the church, with regard to its visible appearance and especially its polity, should now conform to the fundamentals of the newly ruling German nationalist state, to its leadership through the one

3. According to F. Schiller, *Die Verschwörung des Fiesco zu Genua*, V, 16; ET: "Fiesco; or, the Genovese Conspiracy," in F. Schiller, *Romances and Early Dramas* (Boston, 1884), p. 392.

4. R. Sohm, *Kirchenrecht* (Leipzig: Duncker & Humbolt, 1892), vol. 1, p. 533.

5. A. Burgsmüller and R. Weth, eds., *Die Barmer Theologische Erklärung: Einführung und Dokumentation* (Neukirchen-Vluyn: Neukirchener Verlag, 1983), p. 36.

Führer, and to its commitment to the biologically healthy and strong with the exclusion of the racially alien. The centrist part of the church attempted to keep itself largely free of these entanglements by withdrawing into the interior life of the church. But it became clear to their representatives that they could not escape the problem when they had to take a stand on a question in which the National Socialist state was clearly and unmistakably intervening in the interior life of the church: the question of the church's position on Jewish-Christian pastors. In terms of the state's official view, it was unacceptable to have such pastors in the church. The German Christians agreed with this. And the centrist group in the church took as its position a spineless compromise. Martin Niemöller, one of its leaders, declared that on the one hand, such pastors should receive the church's full acknowledgment. But on the other hand, "in view of the 'weakness' that dominates today," they should "exercise the restraint required of them."[6] The church was threatened here by a false doctrine, and its substance was not primarily in the fact that the church was conforming to the *Nazis,* as bad as that was. The true substance of the error was that it *conformed* at all when its eyes should have been focused alone on the head of the church. Because it did not look clearly and frankly at its Lord when dealing with the question of its order and form, the unspiritual organizational question of *church order,* which it more or less conceded to the will or the so-called sense of the masses, became the doorway through which powers that threatened to destroy the church would enter.

3. The Grounded Church

Ephesians 4:15f. teaches us, according to the third Barmen thesis, that the church would not be changed and improved by ethical appeals when dealing with the threat it was to *itself.* It should first of all be put back on its feet and strengthened through its relationship with its head, its source of both comfort and hope. That is the theme of the first of the af-

---

6. K. D. Schmidt, ed., *Die Bekenntnisse und grundsätzlichen Äusserungen zur Kirchenfrage des Jahres 1933* (Göttingen: Vandenhoeck & Ruprecht, 1934), p. 97.

firmative sentences of Thesis Three. The subordinate clause, "in which Jesus Christ acts presently as the Lord," is really the main clause. The church is not grounded by itself. It is not the source of its own continuing life. It is grounded by Jesus Christ. He ensures that that which he has grounded then continues. He does not lie in a grave of the past — and woe to the church that in all seriousness speaks of him in the past tense! It is true that what he has done *once* and for all he need not do again and again, as though he had not done it well enough. He has done it once *for all times*. He is alive. Thus his church has no reason to be arrogant. It cannot step into his place. But it does not have to. Because he *lives*, it need not constantly march in place. The old proposition of the *ecclesia semper reformanda*, which is the concept of the church constantly being renewed, does not mean that the church is constantly to turn its flag toward the wind of the most recent fad. It says that the church is the church *of Jesus Christ* only to the extent that it lives in constant *repentance*, turning away from the idea that Christ is dependent upon the church, turning to the understanding that it is dependent upon him. It is only in that he makes himself present to it that it is the church of Jesus Christ! Its essential dynamic is to move out again and again with the question whether it really is in the place where Christ is now, making himself present.

For that reason, it really has no cause for anxiety and care, neither about its present nor its future, neither about the success of its perhaps frail action nor about its own weakness. It may rely solely on the fact that he is its head and he cares for it. He "gathers, protects, and preserves" his congregation, as the Heidelberg Catechism puts it.[7] If it has no reason for arrogance, then it certainly has no reason for false modesty or for resignation and a lack of courage, especially when it thinks that it has no other option than to give up. It may be courageous — not because it finds its strength in itself, but in the fact that Jesus Christ "acts presently as the Lord" in his church. It may then say, as Martin Luther once said of it, "Fluctuat, non mergitur,"[8] which means, "It may be tossed by the waves but it will not sink," regardless of what people inside and outside the

---

7. Heidelberg Catechism, q. 54, Presbyterian Church (U.S.A.), *Book of Confessions* (Louisville: Office of the General Assembly, 1999), 4.054, p. 37.

8. M. Luther, WA 39 II, 28.26.

church do. That gives us the right to say what this thesis says: If we are *sinners,* then we are nevertheless *sinners blessed by grace,* through Jesus Christ. Through him we are given a new beginning. The sign of this new beginning is the fact that we are incorporated into the Christian church.

In it, "Jesus Christ acts presently as the Lord in Word and Sacrament through the Holy Spirit." In its original form, this sentence was somewhat shorter, stating that in the church "Jesus Christ is proclaimed as Lord."[9] In a commission meeting at the Barmen Synod, Lutheran delegates requested that the sentence should be amended to read that Christ was present in his congregation "in Word and Sacrament." Karl Barth responded: good, but then we will also want to mention the Holy Spirit. When this was agreed to, Wilhelm Niesel, the other Reformed delegate, whispered to Barth, "What a delight for Calvin in heaven."[10] The way the formulation now stands, as Barth later laughingly commented, it is in fact Calvinian solely on the basis of the Lutheran intervention. But he did not understand this as a confessional coup, because he had always understood Calvin to be the model of a union theologian. The point now is this: in that *Jesus Christ* acts presently in the church as its *Lord,* it is "the congregation of the *brothers and sisters.*" They are not that by nature or by some sympathetic feeling. They are so in the way we heard it in Mark 3: because he is in their midst, they are as those gathered around him, brothers and sisters to each other. The New Testament title "brother" was the key term that the Confessing Church then used to counter the racist distinctions that were destroying the common life. There are at other times and places other catchwords with which people, even Christians, may seek to put asunder what God has joined together. Against that, Galatians 3:28 must be asserted: "There is no longer Jew or Greek, there is no longer slave or free, there is no longer male and female; for all of you are *one* in Christ Jesus." We are also reminded here of the unusual term with which the New Testament speaks of Christ as the "firstborn

9. Chr. Barth, *Bekenntnis im Werden: Neue Quellen der Barmer Erklärung* (Neukirchen-Vluyn: Neukirchener Verlag, 1979), p. 59.

10. E. Busch, *Karl Barths Lebenslauf* (München: Chr. Kaiser Verlag, 1975), p. 259; ET: *Karl Barth: His Life from Letters and Autobiographical Texts* (Philadelphia: Fortress, 1976), p. 246.

among many brothers" (Rom. 8:29; see Col. 1:15; Heb. 1:6). This communicates to the members of the congregation the comforting word about how near "our father in heaven" is to them. This is the reason that in the congregation they may be brothers and sisters *to each other.*

4. Commissioned Church

Strengthened by such comfort in view of the church's threat to itself, the power is now given to it to resist this threat and not surrender to it. The second affirmative sentence of Thesis Three deals with this. Just as the biblical text about the body and its head at the beginning of the thesis makes a dual statement — what the head effects in relation to its body, but also what the body, the congregation, must do in its relationship to its head, Christ — the affirmative thesis speaks first of the *grounding* of the church by Christ and then of the *commissioning* of the church by its Lord. What is surprising here is the unusually strong emphasis that the church must testify. But the primary meaning of its testimony is not something to benefit the world around it. That can apparently only be a consequence of what should be its primary testimony, which is, that it is *itself* "*solely* his property." The meaning is clear if we see that the accent here rests entirely on the word "*solely,*" obviously in analogy to the discourse about "the *one* Word" in Thesis One. This "solely" contradicts the church's stance — whether it withdraws or conforms — when it allows itself to be defined, or co-defined, by attentiveness to the dictates of the world. Certainly it cannot and must not act as though these dictates did not exist. What is at stake here is that the church, in the midst of these dictates, should *align itself totally* under the conviction "that it is *solely* his property." Only in this way can it be a light for the world around it, whether constructively or critically. The tone of the first question of the Heidelberg Catechism, already audible in Barmen Thesis One, is recaptured here: "My only comfort is that I *belong* to my faithful Savior, Jesus Christ."[11] There is the church's comfort and at the same time God's claim on it.

11. Question 1.

57

If it is *"solely* his property," then this certainly makes clear that it lives and desires to live *solely* from the comfort of its Lord, but not *merely* from his comfort as though in the *law* the voice of another Lord were speaking, or as though the voice of the divine Lord could be identified with the commands of some earthly authority. Were that so, it would not be "solely *his* property." If it solely belongs to him, then it hears his law, his direction, out of the *same* mouth from which it hears comfort. It hears from him not only comfort, but also instruction, and would be greatly saddened if it did not also hear such instruction from him. We note that in the Barmen theses there is a kind of language game going on. The concepts of law and gospel, which are much too maltreated in the German language, and whose relationship is indeed being addressed here, are restated with other concepts in Barmen, while simultaneously their richness is unpacked. This occurs for example in Thesis Two, where the discourse is about God's affirmation and claim, about God's liberation *from* and liberation *for,* about justification and sanctification; or now in Thesis Three, where the discourse is about comfort and instruction. It is apparent that Thesis Three corresponds here to Thesis Two and applies the latter in such a way that what is distinguished is not divided: the comfort and the instruction of its Lord. And if both *belong* together, then the church must deal with its message and its order in a correspondingly appropriate way. It became clear at that time how disastrous it was that the church had grown blind to this — and the church confessed this contritely in the Barmen Declaration. It is denying its Lord, its message about him, its faith in him, when it arranges its visible order and legal structure according to the spirit and letter of the "world of sin." It recognized then what must never be forgotten, what even today has validity — that only when its external order corresponds to its message does it begin to carry out its task of witness.

But for that very reason, it does not exist in an ideal state; for that very reason it is moving on a path that basically comes from its Lord and leads towards him. Thus, it then goes on to say, Christians testify that they live and desire to live solely from the comfort and the instruction of the Lord *"in the expectation of his appearance."* They believe and obey the one who has already come and is coming today. But he came in lowliness and comes today in concealment. Yet he came and comes now in a way that is full of the promise of his future coming. He will come in visible glory, bringing about the consummation of his kingdom. This kingdom is more than the church and is more than what we now may receive already in faith. It is the removal of all hunger and of all tears, the revelation of the beautiful freedom of the children of God. We are *already* on the road toward it, and we are *still* on the road to it. We have been and we are still awaiting it. For this reason the church cannot be completely at home and rooted anywhere in *this* world. For this reason it must constantly set out on its journey, and open itself up — for the future? No, for the future of *Jesus Christ!* Thus it knows that all its thinking and acting are only preliminary and will soon make way for other preliminaries. At every step of the way, it needs the forgiveness of sins and the encouragement to take the next step — and therefore it does not become resigned at the prospect of the imperfection in which it still finds itself and that its members exhibit over and over again. Rather, in these very difficult circumstances it seeks, while sighing deeply, to do its task as well as it can "in the expectation of the appearance of the Lord." It is precisely in this way that it makes its witness in the midst of the world.

Responsible Church Membership

"You know that the rulers of the Gentiles lord it over them, and their great men exercise authority over them. It shall not be so among you; but whoever would be great among you must be your servant" (Matt. 20:25-26).

The various offices in the church do not establish a dominion of some over the others; on the contrary, they are for the exercise of the ministry entrusted to and enjoined upon the whole congregation.

We reject the false doctrine, as though the church, apart from this ministry, could and were permitted to give to itself, or allow to be given to it, special leaders vested with ruling powers.

Johann Wolfgang von Goethe said once, "No one is more a slave than the person who regards himself as free without being so."[1] He apparently meant that such a person is more a slave than others like him because in his feeling of alleged freedom he no longer knows and senses that he is truly captive and still needs to be liberated. Applying this statement to the Church Struggle, one might consider asserting what Karl Barth in fact wrote: the centrists in the church, as they functioned in 1933, were "even more disturbing" than the German Chris-

---

1. J. W. von Goethe, *Die Wahlverwandtschaften: Aus Ottiliens Tagebuch,* section 2, ch. 5, *Goethe's Werke* (Stuttgart and Tübingen: Cotta, 1828), vol. 17, p. 261; ET: J. W. von Goethe, "Ottilie's Diary," *Elective Affinities,* trans. D. Constantine (Oxford: Oxford University Press, 1994), p. 151.

tians,[2] because the former thought they were so different from the latter, without really being so.

1. Power and Service

Let us think through Goethe's statement in yet another direction! We will do it by placing Jesus' statement in Matthew 20:25 next to it, the text with which Thesis Four begins. "You know that the rulers of the Gentiles lord it over them, and their great men exercise authority over them. It shall not be so among you; but whoever would be great among you must be your servant." Who could regard himself as more free and less a slave than the master who is even a "ruler"? — one who has the power "to enslave the nations," as the biblical text literally says. Such a person considers it freedom to be able to do or not do whatever he wants, to make his wishes into actions! Such a person can do many things, but not one particular thing: serve! It was a confusing obscuration of the facts when an absolutist prince could describe himself as "the first servant of his state."[3]

We should note carefully that Jesus in this text does not abstractly contrast that powerfulness with a lowliness that is ready to serve. To do so would have served entirely the interests of those worldly princes and rulers. Jesus opposes them with another greatness and powerfulness. In this other powerfulness people are able to and actually do, as a matter of course, what those princes and rulers with all their capacity are not able to do: to carry out the office of servant. They do not do this by submitting dumbly and blindly carrying out the commands of other people without contradiction. Serving is the actual form *of their* powerfulness. It is a form of their freedom. They do it responsibly, without shifting their responsibility over to the one in charge. They do it after the model of their Lord Jesus Christ, who is the "Son of Man," superior

---

2. Letter of September 11, 1933, to R. Hupfeld, in E. Busch, ed., *Reformationstag 1933: Dokumente der Begegnung Karl Barths mit dem Pfarrernotbund in Berlin* (Zürich: Theologischer Verlag, 1998), p. 10.

3. Friedrich II of Prussia, *Mémoires de Brandebourg*, in *Oeuvres*, ed. J. D. E. Preuss (Berlin, 1846), p. 123.

to all the powerful, and who came without laying that power aside but demonstrating what it truly is "to serve," as verse 28 in our passage goes on to say. By doing that, he frees us. He frees us to follow him and to share in his freedom so that we, like him, can serve.

During the Barmen Synod, Hans Asmussen, in his lecture introducing the Declaration, exposited the biblical citation of Thesis Four with these words, "Christ is not opposed to the fact that in the realm of the world princes rule and sovereigns have the power. For us as well it is a serious concern that we give due account to this right of the world."[4] It is indeed true that Matthew 20:25f. focuses the congregation's attention on the order within its own house. But the interpretation made by these two sentences gives a false accent to the words of Jesus. It is certainly the case that violent dominion is practiced in the world's space — not only in dictatorships — and it is well known that the church's own space is not entirely free of the desire to do so as well. But the church acts unjustly if it defines such violent dominion when it happens in the world as "justice." When the church hears Jesus saying, "It shall *not* be so among you," then it should welcome the opportunity to send a signal here in favor of free, peaceful, human co-existence in the state as well. The commentator at the Synod, however, directly excluded that option. Thus, at the Synod, there was a process of deviation from the text. There are situations in which the church's confession speaks against its own confessors.

2. The Offices in the Church

The thesis states that there are *"various offices"* in the church. It does not explain this any further but allows us to consider the Düsseldorf "Eklärung zur Gestalt der Kirche" ("Declaration on the Form of the Church") of May 20, 1933, which speaks thematically of the "various offices."[5] It unpacks this in greater detail with the doctrine of the four ser-

4. A. Burgsmüller and R. Weth, eds., *Die Barmer Theologische Erklärung: Einführung und Dokumentation* (Neukirchen-Vluyn: Neukirchener Verlag, 1983), p. 52.

5. W. Niesel, ed., *Bekenntnisschriften und Kirchenordnungen der nach Gottes Wort reformierten Kirche* (Zürich: Evangelischer Verlag, AG Zollikon, 1938, 1985), pp. 327f.

vices in the congregation, that of the pastor and teacher, that of the presbyter, and that of the deacon.[6] This doctrine goes back to Calvin, according to whom the threefold office of Christ as Prophet, Priest, and King finds its correspondence in the three leadership tasks within the congregation: the office of preaching, to which the office of teaching is appended, and further that of diakonia and that of presbyterial order.[7] In the seventeenth century, this doctrine also found its Lutheran advocacy.[8] Whether or not this was adopted or practiced in the various Evangelical churches, the Barmen thesis asserts that the leadership of the church is carried out by "various offices." This leaves room for diverse arrangements of ecclesial leadership. The Calvinian doctrine can still serve as a guideline for examining whether and to what extent the church is following through on its commissions. At the very least it is clear that the task of leadership in the church is distributed onto various shoulders.

What is indisputably excluded is that the church should be led by *"special leaders [Führern]* vested with *ruling powers,"* as the statement of rejection puts it. Whether or not the church gives such leadership to itself or receives it from others, as the text continues, it does not serve any useful purpose and is in fact reprehensible. It is reprehensible because it directly contradicts the biblical witness cited at the beginning. Thesis Four expressly uses the term "Führer," which at that time had been moved to the foreground with such great splendor, and rejects it. "Führer" [= Leader] means that everyone else beneath and behind him constitute the mass of people who have passed on their responsibility to this leader. They are not liable for whatever they do or have done in obedience to the Führer — indeed, obedience is regarded as a good virtue, even if in their obedience they may have been murderers. They do

---

6. The term "Dienst" can be translated "service" or "ministry"; because of the clerical overtones of "ministry," this translation opts for "service" — TR.

7. J. Calvin, *Institutio christianae religionis,* II.15; IV.3.8-9; ET: John Calvin, *Institutes of the Christian Religion,* trans. F. L. Battles, Library of Christian Classics (Philadelphia: Westminster, 1960), II.15; IV.3.8-9.

8. See H. Schmid, *Die Dogmatik der Evangelisch-Lutherischen Kirche, dargestellt und aus den Quellen belegt,* 6th ed. (Frankfurt, 1876), pp. 249-94; ET: *The Doctrinal Theology of the Evangelical Lutheran Church,* 3rd ed., trans. C. A. Hay and H. E. Jacobs (Minneapolis: Augsburg, 1899), pp. 337-76.

not make use of their own rationality but rather act and proceed along their way under the widespread slogan of the day, "Führer, command, we follow you!" This was totally compatible with the worldview of the then Führer Adolf Hitler, who viewed all humanity as divided into two groups by nature: into a small elite of those who are to lead, and the mass of those who are to implement the elite's will.[9] Are there not such leaders still today, even in democratic states? The evil of such leaders is that they, in fact, prevent and ultimately intentionally seek, using every means and televised imagery possible, to hinder *everyone's* being responsible, both the "rulers and the ruled," as Thesis Five puts it.

The concept of a "Christocracy of brothers and sisters," mentioned in the context of the third Barmen thesis, reminds us that the lordship of the heavenly Lord reveals its goodness in that it rejects such irresponsibility. It both lays the foundation for and promotes every effort toward the church's *teaching* differently from societies that are dominated by such leaders. It ensures that within the church, quietly and persistently, a "counter society" will be built up in order to dismantle an irresponsible society. Thesis Four continues this theme by declaring that the offices carried out by persons in the church correspond to the divine head of the church when they do not set aside or remove the responsibility to be carried out by all the other members of the community, but rather ground and establish it. This is the intent of these offices; they urge the community to carry out the service "entrusted to and enjoined upon the whole congregation." The offices in the community are only functioning properly when they refrain from establishing the "dominion of some over the others." This formulation stimulated the discussion of the church as a "community of brothers and sisters free of all rule."

3. The Service of the Laity

If the various offices in the community, properly understood and practiced, are not meant to rule, this obviously does not mean, instead, that

9. Henry Picker, *Hitlers Tischgespräche,* ed. A. Hillgruber [dtv Dokumente 523] (Stuttgart: Seewald, 1976), p. 51.

the laity then should rule the community. What is at stake is the *service* "entrusted to and enjoined upon the *whole* congregation." Thesis Four articulates here a second basic form of proper church order next to the one already expressed in the context of Thesis Three. The stipulation that all are obligated to serve recalls the basic principle of the old Netherlands church order: "No congregation may attain to rank and dominion over others, nor may any pastor, nor elder, nor deacon do so, but all should be cautious at every suspicion and opportunity so to do."[10] The church cannot rule, and there shall be no ruling within it. This is not because "rule" must be something intrinsically wrong, but because in it and for it only one is Lord, the one who in it "acts presently as the Lord" (Thesis Three). But he is the very one who proved his own lordship in that he — as the Lord! — acted as a servant in their midst. As his disciples, the church and thus every member in it can only be a servant.

Christians are servants, not because "serving" is intrinsically such an excellent thing — it can be something shamefully humiliating — but because the church and its members serve *Jesus Christ*. To serve him, in all the effort and exertion and in spite of them, is chiefly a joyful allowance, a permission and honor "entrusted" to it. Only as such is it also an obedient "should" — a task that is "enjoined," a permission to service that is an obligation to serve. If the church serves him, the Lord over all, then everything it does is diakonia: service, the service of God and the service of humanity, the mutual serving of one another and for and with others outside the circle of its fellowship. The community is not in proper order if its laity, instead of serving, seek to be served by clergy who then do so in response to the members' partially or completely non-Christian desires. The community is in good order when its laity participate in the very same service as those of its members who have a special office.

Service here is not an offensive form of captivity, not an insulting subservience, but rather a particular and concrete form of freedom. To serve others, again, does not mean to wait upon them, but rather it means to be free for them, free to stand in support next to them. The concrete fullness of freedom is the freedom to love. This is already ad-

10. Wilhelm Niesel, ed., *Bekenntnisschriften*, p. 279.

dressed in the biblical citation of Ephesians 4:15 in Thesis Three: "Let us speak the truth in love." Such love is ignited by the fact that God, who is love, loves us (1 John 4:10, 16; Eph. 2:4). When speaking of love, we must not forget that it does not arise out of itself but rather in its entire character is a response that is spontaneously evoked. "Whoever is not loved, does not love" (Johann Caspar Lavater). We are ourselves first loved by people, however well they do so, before we love. In spite of all misgivings, that is an illuminating witness to the fact that God certainly loves us before we are even able to recognize it. But God desires that he should be loved by us, and that with him we should love those around us whom he loves. The double commandment of love reminds us of this: to love God with all our heart, with all our soul, with all our strength, and to love our neighbor as ourselves (Matt. 22:37-39) — our neighbor as the one whom God has placed next to us, even if we think, "if only it weren't he," even if he were our enemy (Matt. 5:44). Even when this love is one-sided, it awaits its becoming truly mutual. But it does not wait until the other is ready for it. It loves now in hope of a future fellowship with our neighbor, not by means of overcoming his differentness, but by overcoming our divisiveness and setting aside the hostility. This is what it means to *serve* God and our neighbor *in freedom*.

4. The Maturity of the Laity

The service of the laity as a basic definition of church order is only properly understood and arranged when it is clear that they can and should carry out their service as those who are responsibly mature. If this clarity is lacking, then their serving becomes a waiting upon some earthly superiors. This is the point of Thesis Four: "The various offices in the church do not establish a *dominion* of some over the others; on the contrary, they are for the exercise of the ministry entrusted to and enjoined upon *the whole congregation*." There has constantly been and there still is the dreadful tendency in the church, even the Protestant Church, to concentrate and reduce the church in its essential substance to its "office-bearers." They are those who give, who rule, who speak; and the remaining people, whom we call the congregation, are the passive, the mute, the mere recipients of official activities. At best there are a few whom we call laypeople who become the co-workers of the *pastor.* Or to put it in more modern terms, "the church" is the office-bearer from whom the people can acquire certain religious performances, when they need them, especially those rites that accompany the passages of life. In contrast to that, it cannot be said and learned enough that the *community* will only carry out the service "entrusted and enjoined upon" it when *everyone* in it is taken seriously as a mature and responsible Christian, and when they take themselves seriously as such. They are to be held accountable for their maturity and they will want to be held accountable for it. "The main fruit of the Spirit," according to the Dutch theologian Hendrikus Berkhof, is "that he opens our mouth."[11] For that "chief fruit" to emerge, for the laity to become capable and desirous of being Christians who have something responsible to say, they require guidance and schooling.

These insights are not new. They were already discovered in the Reformation. Martin Luther wrote in 1523, "No one can deny that every Christian has God's Word and is taught by God and anointed to be a priest . . . , as Peter says in 1 Peter 2:9, 'You are the royal priesthood that you might proclaim the virtue of him who called you to his wonderful light.'" A Christian not only has "the right and power to teach God's Word, he is obligated to do so at risk of the loss of his soul and the displeasure of God." When Christians are gathered together, then the "whole community [!] should call one person," who does this in its midst in a special way.[12] The Heidelberg Catechism puts it even more strongly. According to it, to be a Christian means to be a member of Christ who as such participates in the three offices of Christ — prophet,

---

11. H. Berkhof, *Theologie des Heiligen Geistes,* 2nd ed., Neukirchener Studienbücher 7 (Neukirchen-Vluyn: Neukirchener Verlag, 1988), p. 40; ET: *The Doctrine of the Holy Spirit* (Richmond: John Knox, 1964), p. 36.

12. Martin Luther, *Dass eine christliche Versammlung oder Gemeinde Recht und Macht habe, alle Lehre zu beurteilen und Lehrer zu berufen, ein- und abzusetzen: Grund und Ursache aus der Schrift* (1523), WA 11, 411-13; ET: "That a Christian Assembly or Congregation Has the Right and Power to Judge All Teaching and to Call, Appoint, and Dismiss Teachers, Established and Proven by Scripture," *Luther's Works,* vol. 39 (Philadelphia: Fortress, 1970), p. 309.

priest, and king. This participation takes place in such a way that "I may confess his name," "offer myself a living sacrifice of gratitude," and "fight against sin and the devil with a free and good conscience."[13]

It is important that this Reformation insight is transported, in the fourth Barmen thesis, into the life of modern Christianity. In response to the question as to how an individual Christian arrives at such participation in the offices of Christ, Karl Barth's proposal that "baptism" should be understood as "the ordination of every Christian" might be illuminating.[14] This is how it becomes finally clear that the calling to engage in that responsible maturity is not an optional addition to Christian existence but rather an elemental component of it. To be sure, not all Christians have the same gifts and tasks. The Pauline image of the community as body says that the body has very different members, all of which have their indispensable function, and which are all *one* precisely *in* the exercise of their special task. Their differentiation establishes no "dominion of some over the others," but rather the necessity of their dependence upon one another — under their one head, which is not one of them, but rather is the living Jesus Christ. This makes plain that *everyone* in the community has his or her gifts and tasks. The Second Vatican Council put it well in this sense when it spoke of the "apostolate of the laity" and of their active "participation in the salvific sending of the Church itself"; the laity were "especially called to make the church present and effective in those relations where the church can only become the salt of the earth through them."[15] Where their gifts unfold freely, there the church is properly ordered. Only where the "office-bearers" are *laity,* that is, members of the "laos," of the people of God, only where they are also those who receive and listen, and only where those whom we call laity are also *office-bearers,* both giving and sharing, and thus able to practice their office for everyone in the entire community, only then and there does the community express its vitality. There, as the living community, it gives living witness to its living Lord.

13. Heidelberg Catechism, q. 32, *Book of Confessions* (PC [USA]), 4.032.
14. Karl Barth, *KD* IV/4, p. 22 = *CD* IV/4, p. 201.
15. *The Dogmatic Constitution on the Church: Lumen Gentium,* Art. 33.

The Public Worship of God in the Political World

"Fear God. Honor the emperor" *(1 Peter 2:17).*

Scripture tells us that, in the as yet unredeemed world in which the church also exists, the State has by divine appointment the task of providing for justice and peace. [It fulfills this task] by means of the threat and exercise of force, according to the measure of human judgment and human ability. The church acknowledges the benefit of this divine appointment in gratitude and reverence before him. It calls to mind the Kingdom of God, God's commandment and righteousness, and thereby the responsibility both of rulers and of the ruled. It trusts and obeys the power of the Word by which God upholds all things.

We reject the false doctrine, as though the State, over and beyond its special commission, should and could become the single and totalitarian order of human life, thus fulfilling the church's vocation as well.

We reject the false doctrine, as though the church, over and beyond its special commission, should and could appropriate the characteristics, the tasks, and the dignity of the State, thus itself becoming an organ of the State.

The German politician Gustav Heinemann, who was President of the Federal Republic of Germany from 1969 to 1974, was a delegate to the Barmen Confessional Synod in 1934. At a large meeting after the Second World War he made a statement that precisely and concisely summarizes the fifth thesis of Barmen: "Let us respond to the world when it wants to make us fearful: Your lords are leaving, but our Lord is coming."[1] Although their and his lordship take place simultaneously at the present time, they do so oriented in very different directions. Their lordship will end, and his lordship will become apparent to all in the future. Speaking of eternal life in the city of God, it says in Revelation 21:22: "I saw no temple in the city." There is no need of a special temple there anymore because city and temple will be one, because there "God may be all in all" (1 Cor. 15:28). What will then no longer be twofold is now, "in the as yet unredeemed world in which the church also exists," still twofold: the political commonwealth and the community of believers — state and church. The fact that these spheres are separate as two entities demonstrates that we are living in an as yet unredeemed world. It cannot redeem *itself,* but can only *be redeemed* — by God through the Redeemer whom he has sent. Human attempts to deny or to set aside this twofold character of state and church constitute a misfortune for both. That is the good sense of the *doctrine of the two kingdoms* emphasized by the Reformers. But its good sense is only recognized where, at least in the church, one knows that both are in the same hand, in the hand of the One who has revealed his true countenance in Jesus Christ. That may be still widely concealed, but Christians believe that God will one day disclose himself out of that concealment and that his countenance will then be the same as that which he has shown us in Jesus Christ. Then state and church will be one, that is, one in him. Therefore we may and should now trust and rely on the fact that state and church are certainly different now, but are already today in the hands of the same good shepherd. That is the reason why the principle of Acts 5:29 already holds for Christians now: "We ought to obey God rather than men." That is the good sense of the doctrine of the *royal lordship* of Christ. In terms of the history of theology, Barmen Thesis Five is highly significant because it has united these two doctrines in their good sense in a concentrated formulation: the doctrine of the two kingdoms, and the doctrine of the royal lordship of Christ.

---

1. D. Koch, *Heinemann und die Deutschlandfrage,* 2nd ed. (München: Chr. Kaiser Verlag, 1972), p. 155.

1. Against the Arrogance of
the State and the Church

When we approach Thesis Five, we need first of all to ask about the background that provoked its formulation. The two rejection statements address that. They are directed against views that had already been formulated in the nineteenth century. On the one hand, for the philosopher Hegel the state was, as "the reality of the moral idea," the "intrinsically divine." On the other hand, the Heidelberg theologian Richard Rothe wanted to let the church be absorbed into the state. In the former case a divinization of the state was envisioned and in the latter a transformation of the church into the state.[2] But what both had only thought about is what the Evangelical Church began to translate into practice in the first half of the twentieth century, and especially after 1933. This is what the two rejection statements oppose. The first one focuses indirectly on the state in its manifestation at that time, but speaks *directly* against the "false doctrine" that was being advanced in the *church* and strongly advocated by the German Christian movement. The statement is opposed to the doctrine that "the State, over and beyond its special commission, should and could become the single and totalitarian order of human life, thus fulfilling the church's vocation as well." It is clear that the state would only be *directly* refuted once the *church* had refuted and repudiated this doctrine as it was being advocated within its ranks. In point of fact, however, the German Christians opened the church gates to the totalitarian state with its slogan of racially appropriate Christianity, rooted in German blood and soil. According to its guidelines at the end of 1933, "the church of the German people recognizes in the totalitarian claim of the National-Socialist state God's call to family, folk, and state."[3] How could Christians consent to that? The theologian Friedrich Gogarten explained it in this way: In the state's authority God's hard law encounters us. For that reason the authentic state was not the democratic

2. E. Wolf, *Barmen. Kirche zwischen Versuchung und Gnade* (München: Chr. Kaiser Verlag, 1957), p. 140.

3. A. Burgsmüller and R. Weth, eds., *Die Barmer Theologische Erklärung: Einführung und Dokumentation* (Neukirchen-Vluyn: Neukirchener Verlag, 1983), p. 38.

Weimar state but the totalitarian Hitler state.[4] His colleague Emanuel Hirsch explained it this way: In their most inward being, in their *conscience,* Christians were certainly equal to each other, but in their *external* appearance they were completely defined by the folk among which they lived, by their species, their blood, their racial characteristics, and so on.[5] The church's centrist position did not want to see things as radically as the German Christians did, but said instead: It was only all civil life outside of the *church* that was defined in terms of the folk in that way. This was argued with the concept of law in the following way: the state authority represents God's law on earth; it is an *"order"* established by God. Against it no one may trespass, because otherwise disorder would result. It was therefore necessary that unconditional obedience be given to it. The church, on the other hand, preaches the gospel that offers comfort, although without either wanting to change, or being allowed to change the external order.[6] This was not the kind of thought with which Hirsch's radical views could be resisted. Rather, the German Christians, over against the centrists, demonstrated just where the church ends up when it begins to conform its own order to the state's wishes — the outcome is that not only the church's order but also its message is conformed to those wishes.

The second rejection statement is directed against a "false doctrine" that at first glance appears to mean the opposite of the false doctrine just discussed. But we can already notice that the outcome at which both arrive is, in fact, identical. If in the first case the church lets the state suppress its commission, in the second instance the church *itself* surrenders its commission. In the second the church espouses "the false doctrine, as though the church, *over* and *beyond* its special commission, should and could appropriate the characteristics, the tasks, and the dignity of the *State,* thus itself becoming an organ of the State." Initially this refers to

---

4. F. Gogarten, *Einheit von Evangelium und Volkstum?* (Hamburg: Hanseatische Verlagsanstalt, 1933), pp. 14f., 17f., 21.

5. E. Hirsch, *Das kirchliche Wollen der Deutschen Christen* (Berlin-Charlottenburg: Max Grevemeyer, 1933), esp. p. 11.

6. E.g., W. Künneth, "Das Judenproblem und die Kirche," in W. Künneth et al., *Die Nation vor Gott: Zur Botschaft der Kirche im Dritten Reich* (Berlin: Wichern Verlag, 1933), pp. 90-105.

the crude way in which the German Christians attempted to shape the church's organization and its structures, up to and including the form of its worship service, according to the ideals of the German folk and Führer. But the drawing of that boundary was also directed just as much against more subtle endeavors on the part of the German Christians, which were a challenge to the inner-church opposition. They wanted to supplement and perfect through inwardly oriented measures and spiritual reinforcements what the Hitler state had only outwardly addressed.[7] To put it more clearly, the church can certainly also speak politically and may not seek to avoid doing so because its Lord, whom it proclaims, is also the Lord of the world outside the church. The decisive point here is that the church can speak and act politically *only* as *church*, only in its hearing of the Word of God and only in his service. What the second rejection statement repudiates is the "doctrine" that the church, apart from and next to its *one* commission, has *another*, second task, a task related to the state. If it thinks that it really has such a second task, then it has in effect rejected its *one* and *only* commission.

2. The Witness of Scripture

Thesis Five reacts not only to the provocation that was the target of the two rejection statements. That provocation provides the occasion for a thorough and fundamental confessional statement about the relationship of God, and accordingly of the church, to the task of the state. This is what gives the confessional statement the power to articulate those rejection sentences. Thesis Five also begins with a biblical citation, and it emphasizes this scriptural basis by beginning its second section, the affirmative-theological part, with the words, "Scripture tells us. . . ." The background for this emphasis is the real perplexity at the time about the positions against which the rejection statements were directed: How then can you be so sure about all of this?[8] It is at

---

7. See M. Niemöller, . . . *dass wir an ihm bleiben! Sechzehn Dahlemer Predigten* (Berlin: Warneck, 1935), p. 17.

8. E. Wolf, *Barmen*, p. 143.

the same time a raised finger of warning, that with *this* theme we have to pay careful attention to the Scriptures because Christians are especially in danger here of following their own willfully established convictions and principles, uncorrected by the biblical witness, perhaps even protesting that it is all in harmony with the will of God. The Scriptures, understood in their total message and not simply in terms of this or that single passage, tell us that "[w]e must obey God rather than human authority," as John Calvin cited here Acts 5:29.[9] One may speak here appropriately of a "public worship service," which is to take place in the political arena. It is, of course, very different from the church's service of worship. It does not *state* that God wants things to be done in a certain way. What does happen is that in this public service the very same God is served and should be served *in secret,* to whom the glory is *expressly* given in the church's worship.

Thesis Five begins with the quotation of 1 Peter 2:17: "Fear God. Honor the emperor." The citation is not taken from the often-misused thirteenth chapter of Romans, which would have seemed obvious in terms of the Lutheran tradition, or from that passage in Acts 5:29, which was highly esteemed in the Reformed tradition. If we hear 1 Peter 2:17 in its biblical context, then it does, of course, say something similar to Acts 5:29. According to the will of God, Christians act "as free ones," precisely in that they are *God's* "slaves" alone, and thus they are commanded to honor *all people* and to love the brethren, which then leads to "Fear God. Honor the emperor." In this context it becomes very clear that fear, that is, ultimate respect, is what Christians owe *solely* to God and otherwise to no one. That does not mean that the individual persons or the groups who hold governmental power are to be regarded with contempt. They are indeed to be respected, primarily because of the function they have, but they are not to be respected with that ultimate respect that we owe to God alone, but rather in the way that we basically owe every person respect and honor. For that reason they are not removed from criticism. Since they are all subject to the judgment

---

9. J. Calvin, *Institutio christianae religionis* IV.20.32; ET: Calvin, *Institutes of the Christian Religion,* trans. F. L. Battles, Library of Christian Classics (Philadelphia: Westminster, 1960), IV.20.32, p. 1521.

of God and stand or fall with it, people can and sometimes must render a critical assessment of them. But that too is not contempt but rather respect of their person and of their office.

3. The Divine Appointment of the State

The first sentence in the affirmative-theological part of the thesis is especially important. It states first of all that, according to Scripture, the state has a definite task "by divine appointment." The Scriptures tell us something about this. The area of politics is not an autonomous area left unto itself. Because God's assurance is linked to a claim to our *entire* life, this also contains a claim of God in relation to our communal life. Consequently the "civil authority" does not represent the law of God to all those in subjection to it, as was asserted by an older church tradition and as the Lutheran Werner Elert stated in opposition to Barmen Thesis Five. He held that if the political authorities are God's servant, then *they* "say" the command of God to us.[10] But the Barmen thesis states in opposition to this that in the state *everyone* stands under the claim of God. Even if the representatives of the state do not acknowledge this, Christians cannot ignore it. Thus, in relation to the state and as its citizens, they are not to "trust and to obey" the *state* but *God,* as Thesis Five says. According to this thesis, God's claim in the political sphere consists of the divine *appointment* by which the state is instituted for a particular *task.* In contrast to the concept "order," which is illuminated critically in the rejection statement, the concept "appointment" means that the state remains dependent upon the one who has appointed it and can continue to be assessed in terms of the purpose of its appointment. What makes it a legitimate state is not its mere existence, certainly not the apparatus of power at its disposal, but rather its responsible execution of the task for which God has instituted it. When Christians acknowledge the state, that is, its government, then they do so because they acknowledge the task to which the state is called by God's appointment. Since the divine appointment calls the state to such a task, it is

10. E. Wolf, *Barmen,* p. 146.

possible to specify criteria that can be used by anyone to test whether and to what extent the state is a *proper and just* state.

This already suggests that the defined task of the state is a *limited* task. Otherwise it will become a totalitarian state. Only when its task is limited and not limitless is it controllable. The *totalitarian* state, which at that time was not only recognized in the church as given but was welcomed as the normal form of the state by someone like Friedrich Gogarten,[11] is actually as such an illegitimate state from the very outset. Compared with this, the first sentence of the Barmen thesis concretely names three points at which the limited character of state activity becomes visible and noticeable. First, the state carries out its task "in the as yet unredeemed world," in which, incidentally, the church also stands, without being able arrogantly to distance itself from it. The phrase does not merely mean that an authority, a governing state, is needed because the world, or humanity, and thus the church, are all unredeemed. Even if there is something to that interpretation, the rulers are *themselves* part of the unredeemed world, sometimes in such a way that one can see in them and their actions what it means to be unredeemed. It is thus right when others, who grasp and carry out their task in a better way, step in and replace them. Humanity can then take a deep breath. But even here, the world, humanity, and with it the host of politicians stand in need of redemption. Second, even in the best of cases, it is still true that the state, its rulers, and its voting citizens can only judge and act "according to the measure of human judgment and human ability." How often is insight clouded by manipulated information, and how often is human capacity obstructed by the doubt that one can really make a difference! Third, when we look at it carefully, it is not a sign of strength but of weakness when rulers cannot persuade people with clear rulings and reasonable arguments, but rather only "by means of the threat and exercise of force." Later on, Karl Barth wanted to phrase this sentence more carefully and stated that force should only be used in "cases of emergency."[12] But it is evidence of soci-

---

11. Cf. note 4.

12. K. Barth, *Texte zur Barmer Theologischen Erklärung,* ed. M. Rohrkrämer (Zürich: Theologischer Verlag, 1984), pp. 196f.

ety's profound need for redemption that even then one cannot do without it.

Only now does the most important statement appear. The defined task of the state and its government, in spite of the boundaries within which it is carried out, is not to be described negatively. That is the highly positive task "of providing for *justice* and *peace*." These two concepts take up a formula that was already used in the Reformation for the task of the state. Both of them leave room to be understood in a broad and full sense. *Justice* means that all people in the state receive legitimately what is their own and what is needful to them. Whether a state governs justly or not is to be assessed, according to Huldrych Zwingli's inspired formula, by whether the laws "guarantee the protection of law to those who are oppressed even if they have no voice."[13] And according to Jeremiah 9:24, God the Lord exercises grace *and* justice on the earth and is pleased with both. In biblical thought these two are not opposite but belong together; the exploitation and repression of others is not just even if it is legally allowable. In that sense it appears to be reasonable when in 1963 Karl Barth interpreted Thesis Five, all of which he himself had written, with words from Pope John XXIII:[14] "The state is to promote and to care for the *common good* on the basis of *freedom*. There is to be no coercive welfare but rather a welfare that all will seek, desire, and apply."[15] The second term, *peace*, means amicable life together within states and in their relations with one another. This is not merely an armistice that carries within itself the seeds of future conflicts, and in which armaments are being prepared with increasingly sinister and destructive weapons that will have to be tested and disposed of in some way at some time. The ancient Roman saying must be amended to read not "whoever wants peace prepares for war," but "whoever wants peace prepares for peace." And indeed, peace must be *worked for* in the so-called times of peace, for otherwise war will inexorably come some day. The only real peace is *just* peace. It must be struggled for through the re-

13. Zwingli, *Schriften*, vol. 2, ed. Th. Brunnschweiler et al. (Zürich: Theologischer Verlag, 1995), p. 371.

14. See the encyclicals of Pope John XXIII, *Mater et magistra* (1961), no. 65; *Pacem in terris* (1963), no. 55-57.

15. K. Barth, *Texte*, p. 200.

moval of the causes of conflicts and through peaceful conflict resolution wherever possible. According to Thesis Five, it is part of the blessing of the divine appointment that the state also has access to "the exercise of force." But it is not the possession of power that makes a state into a just state. Its power is only legitimate when it serves justice and peace. It has that power only to inhibit the power of the powerful and to protect the weak from them. It has it only so that justice and peace may rule in the state and among the states. When we understand the power of the state in this way, then we face the question that is not directly articulated by the fifth Barmen thesis. That is the question of the restriction of the state's power over against the danger of its becoming too powerful. The normal form of the restriction is provided by the democratic state; the extraordinary form is the elimination of a tyranny by assassination of the despot.

4. The Church's Relationship to the Political Sphere

After the first two sentences of the affirmative section of this thesis have discussed *God's* relation to the state, that is, its appointment by him, the next three sentences discuss how then the *church's* relation to the state is to be structured in the light of God's relation to the state. The first sentence begins with a surprise. According to the theological practice of that time, this would have been the place to speak of the *law,* or more precisely, of the external use of the law, which means the requirement of obedience for Christians as well. The placement of the gospel before the law in Thesis Two has its effect here, in that the first thing mentioned is the *benefit* to be received "in gratitude and reverence before [God]." This gratitude and reverence are not related to the condition of a particular state, and certainly not to the quality of the office-bearers within a state at any given time. They are related neither to people nor to human institutions. They are related to the *divine appointment* standing behind them, the appointment that is believed in and acknowledged as divine. Respectful gratitude does not exclude, under certain circumstances, criticism of the state and its representatives, nor does it rule out opposition and resistance to it. What it does exclude is that a corrupt state should be replaced by something other than a *state*. We must be very precise here: the fact that a state has power does not mean that it is corrupt. Jacob Burckhardt's axiom, "power is in itself evil,"[16] is famous but not correct. One easily concludes that the temptation to abuse power always lurks close to power itself. But it must be stated that the *wrong* use of power is what is evil. The benefit of God's appointment requires that such a distinction be made. By such appointment God ensures that governments exist in earthly life with the task of providing for justice and peace in an as yet unredeemed world.

The next sentence in Thesis Five does then speak of the *law* or "command," but again in a surprisingly different way from what was the theological custom at the time. It is not the actual order of the state that constitutes the law that applies to everyone, including Christians. As a result of placing the gospel before the law, the way of speaking of the law is completely different. It is the law *of God* that encounters humans, in distinction from all other legal orders. Its character is illumined by the gospel that precedes it, so that no threat is made with it, but rather it "calls to [our] mind" what just action is. And it is not *merely* command, but is framed and interpreted by the terms "kingdom of God" and "God's righteousness." Thus it does not enforce submission and allegiance, but instead calls for responsibility. It is not that God's command comes through the rulers to the ruled, so that the ruled owe obedience to the rulers. The critical opponent of the declaration, the Lutheran theologian Werner Elert, in his introduction to the theses at the Barmen Synod, saw more clearly than did Hans Asmussen himself that this was precisely what Thesis Five ruled out.[17] Rather, *both*, the rulers and the ruled, are made *accountable* in the same way. When the church, addressing both, "calls [this] to mind," in effect a barrier is erected against both the autonomy of the state and the mentality of passive subjection on the part of the people. The fact that the *church* calls this to mind makes it clear that it does intervene in the po-

16. J. Burckhardt, *Weltgeschichtliche Betrachtungen, Gesammelte Werke* IV (Darmstadt, 1956), p. 25; ET: *Force and Freedom: Reflections on History* (New York: Pantheon, 1943), p. 115.

17. Wolf, *Barmen*, p. 146; about Asmussen, see Barth, *Texte zur Barmer Theologische Erklärung*, p. 54.

litical world and exercise a "prophetic sentinel's office," without ceasing to be the church. The Lutheran theologian in Erlangen, Paul Althaus, criticized this passage as being the "political concept of the . . . liberal state under the rule of law" and no longer that of the new authoritarian order of the German folk.[18] It is indeed quite true that the entire thesis emerges as a supportive argument for the democratic state under the law. Democracy on these terms is something more than merely ascertaining majorities. It has not been fully realized if that is all that it means. Democracy means that all responsible parties participate in the decision-making process for the organization of the common good. Democracy also means the right to oppose and the protection of minorities from the majorities' abuse of power. Democracy means resistance against a disempowerment like that about which Karl Marx wrote: "The worker will become a cheaper product the more he produces."[19] Democracy means uncensored and unmanipulated public expression of opinion and public control of the concentration of power in economy, finance, and the media — as per Alexander Solzhenitsyn's admonition, "Let us not forget that violence does not and cannot flourish by itself; it is inevitably intertwined with lying."[20] And violence rules according to George Orwell's phrase: "Big brother is watching you." It is part of the political sentinel's office of the church to "call to mind" that right of common responsibility. The church is not acting counter to its commission when it is engaged in political affairs in that way.

In doing so, it "trusts and obeys the power of the Word by which God upholds all things." That is how it is put in the last sentence of the first section of Thesis Five. The concepts "trusting and obeying" relate this statement back to Thesis One, according to which we as Christians are to trust and obey the *one* Word of God. In the practice of political responsibility, too, we are firstly and finally bound only to this *one* Word. Now it says, however, that through this one Word God upholds

18. C. Nicolaisen, *Der Weg nach Barmen. Die Entstehungsgeschichte der theologischen Erklärung von 1934* (Neukirchen-Vluyn: Neukirchener Verlag, 1985), p. 88.

19. K. Marx, *Einleitung der Kritik der politischen Ökonomie* (1859).

20. Alexander Solzhenitsyn, Nobel Prize Speech, 1970, see www.columbia.edu/cu/augustine/arch/solzhenitsyn/nobel-lit1970.htm.

"all things." This statement is a citation from Hebrews 1:3, although without referring to it, and it also reminds us of Ephesians 1:21, where Christ is raised up "far above all rule and authority and power and dominion." We hear these citations next to the word from 1 Peter 2:17 with which Thesis Five begins: "Fear God. Honor the emperor." It thus becomes clear why ultimate respect is due only to God and why he shares his glory with no power on earth, however mighty it might be. This is because "God upholds all things" and thus has them in his hand, including the powerful. At the same time, this citation refers back to the previous three sentences in the thesis. If it is true as stated there that the state by divine appointment has the task to provide for justice and peace, and if furthermore the church acknowledges the benefit of this appointment, and if finally it summons all to political responsibility by recalling God's kingdom, command, and righteousness, then all of that is not arbitrary game-playing and not an aberration from its actual task. The legitimate *grounds* for the political duty of the church *as* church is "the power of the Word by which God upholds all things," and through which God moves his church to trust and to obey it. The church father Athanasius, speaking once in a time of genuine threat, said boldly, *nubicula est, transibit* ("this is a little cloud that will pass").[21] One is reminded of this when the church in 1934 was able to make this confident confession in view of the overwhelmingly impressive apparatus of power and in spite of the church's profound failure in response to it: "all things," even the triumphal rhetoric of the worldly ruler, are no competitors for God. And also in our failure nothing is able to take us away from him. "All things" are upheld by him and are all in his hand.

* * *

To return now to the beginning of the lecture: the strength of Barmen's Thesis Five is that it interrelates the good meaning of the doctrine of two kingdoms and of the royal lordship of Christ. We must now add to this that it also simultaneously rules out the problematic meaning of

21. Rufinus, *Historia ecclesiae,* I, 34.

these two doctrines. In 1933 it was primarily a problematic meaning of the two kingdoms doctrine that came to the fore. The *proper* sense of that doctrine is its emphasis that *God* rules the church, so that the church must allow itself to be ruled by God rather than man in every dimension, including its relationship to the state, thus obeying God rather than man in accordance with Acts 5:29. This doctrine is *wrongly* accented if it is expounded to mean that the church must only attend to its inner affairs while the external things, the things of the world, which it does not understand anyway, are not its concern. That is certainly wrong. For even if all it can do for these external things is *pray* about them in its worship, it is *by doing so* making itself responsible for them.

The doctrine of the royal lordship of Christ, on the other hand, has its *proper* meaning in the emphasis that the same God who rules the church also rules secretly over the rest of the world, and thus over the state that surrounds the church. This correct statement becomes *false* if it is interpreted to mean that the lordship of Christ in some way also permits the *church* to exercise lordship over the state. Behind this interpretation is often the mistrust that God is not carrying out his task with regard to the political world well enough, and the church needs to come to his assistance. It is certainly true that the church should be the *witness* to the will and action of God in relation to the political world. But as such a witness it cannot be or become ruler, but must be and remain servant. As such it cannot from time to time put its calling to the service of God on hold in order to pursue its own interests by devoting itself to a part-time job as a political power or opposition. Rather, the more it endeavors as church to be *proper* church, the better it can invite and encourage the state to be *proper* state.

I conclude by repeating the entire text of Thesis Five of the Barmen Declaration:

> *"Fear God. Honor the emperor."*
>   *Scripture tells us that, in the as yet unredeemed world in which the church also exists, the State has by divine appointment the task of providing for justice and peace. [It fulfills this task] by means of the threat and exercise of force, according to the measure of human judgment and*

84

human ability. The church acknowledges the benefit of this divine appointment in gratitude and reverence before him. It calls to mind the Kingdom of God, God's commandment and righteousness, and thereby the responsibility both of rulers and of the ruled. It trusts and obeys the power of the Word by which God upholds all things.

We reject the false doctrine, as though the State, over and beyond its special commission, should and could become the single and totalitarian order of human life, thus fulfilling the church's vocation as well.

We reject the false doctrine, as though the church, over and beyond its special commission, should and could appropriate the characteristics, the tasks, and the dignity of the State, thus itself becoming an organ of the state.

The Mission of the Church in the World of Religion

"Lo, I am with you always, to the close of the age" (Matt. 28:20). "The word of God is not fettered" (2 Timothy 2:9).

The church's commission, upon which its freedom is founded, consists in delivering the message of the free grace of God to all people in Christ's stead, and therefore in the ministry of his own Word and work through sermon and Sacrament.

We reject the false doctrine, as though the church in human arrogance could place the Word and work of the Lord in the service of any arbitrarily chosen desires, purposes, and plans.

"Methinks I scent the morning air," says the Ghost in Shakespeare's *Hamlet*.[1] When Christians scent the morning air, they will get up and break camp. They will go out to others in the hope that they too will awaken and scent the morning air. The Dutch theologian Hendrikus Berkhof said, "The great danger of the church all over the world is indeed the danger of introversion. As soon as that is her attitude, she shirks her calling to participate in the great movement from the One to the universe; she becomes static and, as such, disobedient." Berkhof then cited 1 Peter 2:9, "You are . . . God's own people, that you may declare the wonderful deeds of him who called you out of darkness into his marvelous light."[2] This is what the sixth thesis of the Barmen Declaration is speaking about.

1. W. Shakespeare, *Hamlet*, Act I, Scene 5.
2. Hendrikus Berkhof, *Theologie des Heiligen Geistes*, 2nd ed. (Neukirchen-Vluyn:

If the fifth Barmen thesis deals with the relationship of the church to the *state,* then the sixth Barmen thesis deals with the relationship of the Christian movement to *non-Christians.* If Thesis Five speaks of the *political* service of God, then Thesis Six speaks of the *missionary* service of God. This is a notable fact. In our church world these are two themes that, if they are dealt with at all, are often played off against each other, or approached as though one had the option to choose between the one or the other. Over there the more progressive ones are engaged with the political service of God, and over here the more conservative ones devote their efforts to the mission of the church. Both tasks are indeed falsely understood if they are separated and played off against each other. In this regard as well the Barmen Declaration is a significant church document because in it both actions are connected to each other. The fundamental point it makes for us is that the one task can only be done properly when the other is done as well. This is the two-fold form of the church's sending into the world around it as well as to the fellow humans of its age.

As far as *mission* is especially concerned, there were two dominant conceptions in the period before the Barmen Synod, both of them reaching back to the nineteenth century.[3] The one was that the "heathens" were to become Christians through the call to personal conversion. According to the other view of mission, the "heathens" should be persuaded of the superiority of Christianity through cultural and civilizing endeavors. Both conceptions could prove meaningful, and both could be connected to each other in such things as medical services. But both became dangers when, in the course of mission, the *haves* dominated the *have-nots,* and tended to think that it is not we but rather the others who should get converted and improve their lot. Then the Christians did not do the one thing commanded of them, which is to stand in the service of Christ. This problem appeared to have been dealt with by the doctrine of mission that emerged in the

---

Neukirchener Verlag, 1988), p. 44; ET: *The Doctrine of the Holy Spirit* (Richmond, VA: John Knox, 1964), p. 39. [These were the Warfield Lectures in 1964 — TR.]

3. See K. Barth, "Die Theologie und die Mission in der Gegenwart" (1943), in *Theologische Fragen und Antworten. Gesammelte Vorträge,* vol. 3 (Zürich: Zollikon, 1957), pp. 118ff.

1920s.[4] It emphasized that the disciples are sent to "all *nations*" according to Matthew 28:19. Included in this emphasis, according to this doctrine of mission, was the task of adapting the proclamation totally to the distinctive situations of the diverse nations. But there is a difference — a serious difference like the one between truth and error — whether one says that the God normatively testified to in the Bible loves in a wonderful way *all people* in their various ethnicities, or one says that rootedness in a distinctive people is the inviolable presupposition for one's being loved by God and for the proclamation of that love. *And* there is also a difference whether, because of this love, people break out of the life they have been leading, as Abraham left his people and moved out to the land that God would show him, or whether, based on their interpretation of this love they are simply encouraged to continue living their customary lives but in a somewhat improved way. In the first instance, we are speaking of God's unconditional and free *grace,* and in the second, of a naturally given human *precondition* for his grace. In 1933 this problem was profoundly exacerbated.

1. The Concept of "National Mission" in the Year 1933

In the twentieth century this concept was in the air in the decade of the thirties. The German concept "Volksmission," or "national mission," had been coined a short time before and could be defined in a variety of ways. It could mean that the time of mission among the "faraway heathen" was now past because the churches that had been established in the various parts of the world could take over the task independently. These were churches with whom we now live in ecumenical fellowship. Perhaps they now have even a missionary task in our no longer so very Christian countries because mission to and among *our* people has become an urgent matter. But "national mission" can also mean something very different. This becomes plain when we ask what this slogan of national mission meant in Germany in 1933, when many Christians were claiming that it had become necessary. The term emerges in an

4. See Barth, "Die Theologie und die Mission in der Gegenwart," p. 120.

emphatic way in the rhetoric of the German Christian movement. The administration of their imperial church, the *Reichskirche,* made an appeal for national mission and published the following guideline for it in November 1933: "All those working in national mission must be both clearly grounded in the gospel and persuaded members of the Third Reich." It was in this sense that the notorious Berlin Sport Palace Rally, which took place shortly thereafter, was conceived of as a "*national mission* event."[5] And it was entirely consistent when they appealed there for "liberation from the Old Testament" and for its replacement with stories of a "Germanic kind."[6] The rootedness of the earliest Christians in the people of Israel was to be repealed today by one's rootedness in the German people. In 1932 the German Christians had already declared that, although they did not want to "tamper with the confessional foundation of the Evangelical Church," they wanted nevertheless to supplement this foundation with this "living confession." "We want an evangelical church that is rooted in nationhood [!]" and protects the nation from the "degeneration of our people."[7] The *root* of that kind of national mission is not the gospel but openly and avowedly Germanic nationhood, and the gospel here apparently does not have the power to hinder the expulsion of the racially impure from the Germanic people.

The same slogan, "national mission," was also important to the internal church opposition to the German Christians. After they lost the church elections to the German Christians in July 1933, they applied themselves seriously to what they called "comprehensive national mission efforts."[8] What they meant by this was similar to the German Christians: this work should take place in the framework of their church programmatic strategy, whose thrust was that they devote themselves to "the inner strengthening of the people" in the "uncompromising service of the German nation."[9] Even Dietrich Bonhoeffer, writing in a preparatory document for the Bethel Confession, stated

---

5. J. Gauger, *Chronik der Kirchenwirren,* vol. 1 (Elberfeld: privately published, 1934), p. 108.

6. Gauger, *Chronik der Kirchenwirren,* p. 109.

7. Gauger, *Chronik der Kirchenwirren,* p. 67.

8. Gauger, *Chronik der Kirchenwirren,* p. 96.

9. Gauger, *Chronik der Kirchenwirren,* p. 77.

that the church "enters with its proclamation and in its external forms into the various peoples." To be sure, its "adaptation to the people . . . reaches its boundary at the content of the gospel." But how clear can that boundary be if one then goes on to say that the church must become "German to the Germans"? Why *must* it? Because, he says, "the church . . . never [hovers] over the peoples. It lives *within* the peoples."[10] This is said more clearly by the Bethel Confession, published soon thereafter by that internal church opposition to the German Christians: "The people of a certain nation, who are at the same time members of the church that lives in this nation, are inseparably bound to both." It is virtually rejected as heresy, then, to state that the church "in its structure and proclamation does not have to pay attention to the distinctive character of a particular nationhood."[11] One should consider that this was being said in a time in which it was legally required that church proclamation must give "careful consideration" to racially defined nationhood! When the Augsburg Confessional Synod then established an "office for national mission," its rationale was that the church would be making here its "contribution" to the widespread "serious efforts for the restructuring of the German character"; this was the task of "the German conscience awakened in the Reformation to the awareness of its responsibility for nation and fatherland."[12]

This was the approach that the spokesman for the inner-church opposition, Martin Niemöller, widely and publicly advocated in his sermons. The national "rebirth" emerging in politics would really become a blessing for "our German nation," when it is "inwardly supported by a revival of the Christian faith."[13] Was the church, then, in its inner upbuilding of the German nation through its national mission, only providing the ritual oil to lubricate the better functioning of the state's welcome endeavor to generate a rebirth of the nation? A church under-

---

10. D. Bonhoeffer, *Gesammelte Schriften,* vol. 2, ed. E. Bethge (München: Chr. Kaiser Verlag, 1965), p. 112.

11. M. Niemöller, ed., *Das Bekenntnis der Väter und die bekennende Gemeinde* (München: Chr. Kaiser Verlag, 1933), p. 32, 29.

12. Gauger, *Chronik der Kirchenwirren,* p. 545.

13. M. Niemöller, . . . *dass wir an ihm bleiben! Sechzehn Dahlemer Predigten* (Berlin: Warneck, 1935), p. 17.

stood in that way is apparently required then to let its national mission be bound and shaped by the alleged distinctive features of Germanic nationhood. Accordingly, Niemöller, in his "Propositions on the Aryan Question in the Church," came to the defense of the so-called "non-Aryan" pastors. But he still found them to be a "burden" for the church in its *national mission* and expected "self-restraint" from them — without explaining just what he really meant by that.[14] It is not possible to come to any other conclusion but that Jewish-Christian pastors, for allegedly biological reasons, should not participate in a major church event, even though the pretense was that they were to be defended.

2. The Objection of the Sixth Barmen Thesis

When, one year after the Barmen Synod, the Augsburg Confessional Synod of 1935 spoke about national mission in the fashion just cited, it was clearly contradicting Barmen's sixth thesis. It did not go unnoticed that this thesis distanced itself from those views of national mission. Just a few days *before* the Barmen Synod, the theologian Paul Althaus commented "that in the entire draft the term 'People' [Volk] does not occur except in Thesis Six. . . . There happily the word *People* [Volk] is mentioned in the phrase 'to all people'. But it is not the concept in our sense" — that is, as a claim relevant to "the life necessities . . . of our *[German]* nation . . . but rather as a non-binding biblical expression"[15] taken from Luke 2:10! The Bavarian Bishop Meiser concurred: "The declaration is silent regarding proclamation that is *appropriate for our nationhood.*"[16] He then had his theological advisor draft a revised version of the sixth thesis to convey the sense of that folk-based understanding of national mission, which affirmed that the German Evangelical Church knew itself to be called to "joyful service of the German nation."[17]

14. *Junge Kirche* 1 (1933): 269-71.
15. C. Nicolaisen, *Der Weg nach Barmen. Die Entstehungsgeschichte der theologischen Erklärung von 1934* (Neukirchen-Vluyn: Neukirchener Verlag, 1985), pp. 87f.
16. Nicolaisen, *Der Weg nach Barmen*, p. 92.
17. Nicolaisen, *Der Weg nach Barmen*, p. 191.

The sixth Barmen thesis contradicts the view under discussion by looking far beyond the dominant understanding of German national mission in 1933, which prescribed that proclamation should be conformed to German nationhood. In its rejection statement, it opposes *every* attempt to carry out the "church's commission" and thus its mission in such a way that "the church in human arrogance could place the Word and work of the Lord in the service of any arbitrarily chosen desires, purposes, and plans." The error is not the question of engaging people in such a way that they understand the gospel. The gospel itself has both the will and the power to create a hearing for itself in every language and people, and when that happens, it demonstrates the will and the power of the *gospel* and not its dependence upon anthropological concessions. The fundamental error is that the church in its mission is not subjecting *itself* to the Word of its Lord but rather it subjects *his Word* to intentions that it has established and is striving for, completely apart from his Word. Its error is that it does not carry out its task as service *solely* of the "Word and work of the Lord," but that it uses the Word and work of the Lord to bless interests that it has formulated without listening to the Word of God.

This can happen in subtle ways, perhaps with assurances that one wants merely to take note of the needs of one's addressees for the sake of the greater success of the message, or so that the message is not experienced by them as coercion. Can one imagine what would have happened to the words of the Old Testament prophets or to the preaching of the Apostle Paul if they had been subjected to this kind of intention! What the messengers regard as the needs of their contemporaries becomes ultimately the standard for what the "Word and work of the Lord" can give them, and what it cannot do for them. Ultimately the only message the church can endorse is one that, according to the church's representatives, will be acceptable and pleasing to the people. This means that the message is being put into the service of human interests. Certainly there are well-intentioned arbitrary "desires, purposes, and plans" next to those evil ones arbitrarily selected! But to place the Word and work of the Lord at the service of either is certainly arbitrary. The issue is not that such usage of the message should be done in humility rather than in "human arrogance." That the church thinks it has the Word and work of the Lord at its disposal and can adapt it to whichever human desires, purposes, and plans it chooses, *that* is ecclesial "arrogance." This arrogance means that the church, the official church, is not in the *service* of its benevolent Lord, but it has the *ruling position* between God and humanity.

3. Biblical Clarification

The sixth Barmen thesis counters this with two biblical citations. The first says, "Lo, I am with you always, to the close of the age." This reminds us of the *entire* Great Commission in Matthew 28:18-20. This commission not only mandates proclamation to "all nations." It also mandates what this proclamation shall accomplish with its hearers, namely, their becoming *disciples of Jesus.* According to Acts 1:8, the mission command is even a description of their life as disciples of Jesus: "You *will be* my witnesses." That is as obvious as the fact that one cannot be a Christian without believing in Christ. The sixth thesis expressly cites only the promise, given with the Great Commission, that the Ascended One will be present to his church in all ages and at all places. This promise is the light that illumines the congregation as it obeys the Great Commission. In fact, the promise shifts the missionary mandate into the proper light. For if Christ is with you "always," then *he* is the chief missionary. He will then validate his own Word and work in such a way that we may not be so self-confident or so worried as to think that nothing would happen if *we* are not the representatives of an absent Christ. To be sure, that commission describes us in 2 Corinthians 5:20 as messengers "in Christ's stead," as cited in the positive confessional statement, but this means that we do this in his *"service"* — in the service of his Word spoken by him and his work made effective by him. *Then* the church is not acting in arrogance but rather as a company of God's servants and Jesus' followers, who unobtrusively but still clearly invite people to be reconciled with God.

The second biblical citation is taken from 2 Timothy 2:9. Heinrich Bullinger quoted the same verse in 1531 when the Zurich government wanted to impose regulations for the church's preaching on him: "The word of God is not fettered."[18] This Word, first of all, is superior to a danger with which its Christian messengers can threaten it. They could fetter the Word in such a way that it no longer is permitted to say what it *wants* to say, but rather what it is *supposed* to say according to "arbitrarily chosen desires, purposes, and plans." The biblical quotation confesses the power of God's Word over against this danger. We do not have this Word in our hand; we are in its hand. Step by step we continue to be dependent upon its opening itself to us as it does to others. By virtue of its visible demonstrations of power, it *will* do that, often where we do not expect it, and perhaps not at the very place where we would like to fit it to our wishes and plans — not to "race, folk, and nation," as the German Christians declared at that time. Instead it will bind itself to the "incompetents and the inferiors" whom the German Christians wanted to get rid of.[19] By virtue of its power, however, there is the hope that this Word does in fact engage "*all* people." And thus we may be confident that this Word is also more powerful than the danger that threatens it *from outside of the church*. There, they may not so much want to reject the Word, but rather silence it more effectively by muzzling it like a dancing bear, binding it with a chain and letting it dance its practiced routine. They do not contest it. But they make the gospel into the very thing that Karl Marx criticized: "Religion is the opium of the people."[20] Sometimes demanding, sometimes smiling, they demand that the Word of God should bless and not disturb the arbitrary acts of humans. Its messengers, then, certainly do not end up in prison, as foreseen in 2 Timothy 2:9 — which means that they do not bear the disgrace of Christ (Heb. 13:13), nor do they follow him by taking up his cross (Matt. 16:24), but rather become public figures who are far too popular — not because they make such an impression with the Word of

18. See, e.g., "Bullingers Verteidigung der freien Predigt des Gotteswortes (1531)," in C. Pestalozzi, *Heinrich Bullinger. Leben und ausgewählte Schriften* (Elberfeld, 1858), pp. 74ff.

19. A. Burgsmüller and R. Weth, eds., *Die Barmer Theologische Erklärung. Einführung und Dokumentation* (Neukirchen-Vluyn: Neukirchener Verlag, 1983), p. 35.

20. K. Marx, *Zur Kritik der Hegelschen Rechtsphilosophie,* 1843; ET: "Excerpt from Toward the Critique of Hegel's Philosophy of Right," in L. S. Feuer, ed., *Basic Writings on Politics and Philosophy: Karl Marx and Friedrich Engels* (Garden City, NY: Doubleday, 1959), p. 263.

God but rather because they are willing to submit so cooperatively to that human arbitrariness.

4. The Church's Commission

According to the positive confessional statement of the sixth thesis, the "church's commission" is "delivering the message of the free grace of God to all people." There is an allusion here to the "great joy" which according to Luke 2:10 is "to be to *all* people" — Huldrych Zwingli commented on this, "Never has the world received more joyful news."[21] If the proclamation is not allowed to be placed in the service of arbitrary interests, then the people are not offered stones instead of bread (Matt. 7:9). They then receive what they *really* need and not just appear to need, what does not produce for them new frustration but rather genuine joy. It is *that* joy that does not cease when there are burdens to be borne. It is *that* joy for the sake of which God made himself into our servant in Christ.

Instead of great joy, the thesis speaks of *"free grace,"* and this phrase then has its own particular accent. Free grace means that we cannot bind it to ourselves. It binds itself to us and us to it. Free grace means that no person has an innate spiritual antenna for it. If nonetheless it reaches us, then that is only because God allows it to reach us. Free grace also means that no person possesses the innate power of resistance to obstruct it if it wants to enter into one's life. Concretely, free grace means that God has chosen from all the peoples only one, Israel, to be his people, and that it is clearly free, overflowing, and rich grace when it also reaches out to persons from all the peoples. Free grace also contains a No to man, since he has not merited God's turning to him. Unless he separates himself from his arbitrarily selected wishes, goals, and plans, he will not grasp it. But God's No is not without his Yes. In it he affirms his love for us and tells us that we are lost if he does not love us in his free grace. Free grace means, finally, that it is not within

21. H. Zwingli, *Schriften,* vol. 2, ed. Th. Brunnschweiler et al. (Zürich: Theologischer Verlag, 1995), p. 43; ET: "The Defense of the Reformed Faith," in *Huldrych Zwingli: Writings,* trans. E. J. Furcha (Allison Park, PA: Pickwick, 1984), p. 26.

our competence to reach out to *others* in the process of mission. At most we can be witnesses of the fact that *God* in his grace is free to disclose himself to others aside from us.

The word "freedom" occurs in the sixth thesis a second time. Now it is oriented towards the *church.* The free church corresponds to free grace. One aspect of this correspondence is that in both instances the issue is not an arbitrary freedom without any bonds. Just as God is free in his *grace,* the church too is free in *its commission.* The thesis basically says that the freedom of the church is *"grounded"* in its commission. If, instead of serving him, it put the Word and work of the Lord "in the service of any arbitrarily chosen desires, purposes, and plans," then it is only *apparently* free. In fact, it loses its freedom in the process. It will exhaust itself with its efforts to satisfy people's needs as they are manipulated by the media. It will, for its part, become slave and prisoner of old and new forms of human arbitrariness. The freedom of the church cannot persist if it is separated from its commission. Its commission consists of its serving the Word and work of Jesus Christ. It is free *only* in this commission. But it is truly *free* in it, free in a double sense. It is, for one, free of having to be a slave of humans, as Paul notes in Galatians 1:10. For another, because the performance of Christ's "own Word and work" is solely his affair and not that of Christians, they are then free to respond to him humanly with their "*own* word and work." In both instances the freedom is *bound* to the *commission* to make known the message of "free grace." This indicates the limits for the extent to which the messengers should adapt themselves to their addressees when making the message known, or vice versa. The limit consists of the fact that both, the messengers and their addressees, *together* must *begin* anew to hear this message.

Thesis Six says that the spread of the message happens decisively "through sermon and Sacrament." This does not mean that the mission of the church is a one-hour program conducted by the pastor on Sunday morning, in the presence of a company of laity who listen quietly to him or her. It would be difficult to claim that this assemblage represents "all the people" to which the message of free grace is to be proclaimed. Rather, we must understand these terms in a more fundamental way, with a dual sense. First, we should understand every missional endeavor as a kind of *worship event*, and not merely as a dialogue to facilitate the mutual acquaintanceship of "Christianity" and the other religions. We would not be taking missionary service as seriously as it must be taken if it did not have at its center the focus on the gospel and on table fellowship in the presence of Christ. In its mission, the church does paradigmatically what it does again and again in "sermon and Sacrament." "In mission the church risks doing the same thing that it otherwise risks in the form of repetition, now in the form of beginnings."[22] Second, every Sunday worship service of the congregation must be understood and carried out as a "missional event." The act of public worship is a pause to take a breath on the *entire* congregation's pathway of sending. The community is not "dismissed" at the end of public worship with the blessing of the Lord, but is rather *sent out* with the blessing of the Lord. It is sent out not so much so that each one can do one's duty in one's earthly vocation, as Albrecht Ritschl thought in the nineteenth century,[23] but rather so that each one *in and under and alongside of* one's vocation might love and serve God among one's contemporaries who are alienated from God.

5. The Addressee of Mission

According to Thesis Six, the addressee is "all people." To put it in a pointed way, the actual addressee of the free grace of God is not the church, but rather "all people." The church can only be the *witness* to this. If it also wants to be the *addressee* of God's free grace, then it can only do so in solidarity with "all people." It is just as much in need of forgiveness as are all the rest, and it knows at the same time that as God loves it in spite of that, God also loves all the *others* who do not know it yet. The Bible understands the word "all" here very concretely, and thereby corrects a concept of "people" in which there are always those

22. Barth, "Die Theologie und die Mission in der Gegenwart," p. 101.

23. A. Ritschl, *Die christliche Lehre von der Rechtfertigung und Versöhnung*, 4th ed. (Bonn: Adolph Marcus, 1895), vol. 3, pp. 420ff., 556; A. Ritschl, *The Christian Doctrine of Justification and Reconciliation*, ed. and trans. H. R. Mackintosh and A. B. Macaulay (Edinburgh: T. & T. Clark, 1902).

who are located at the bottom or on the outside. The "great joy" of Luke 2 was announced *first of all* to the shepherds, to those located at the bottom or outside, and only in this way was the promise made that this good news was "for all the people." What happened there reflects again God's free grace. By reaching first of all those who stand at the margins, it validates the fact that it is the message that is "for *all*." In Christ, the Word of God became *human*. This is not intended to transform the world into the church, but to redeem the world in the kingdom of God. That does not render the church superfluous. But it does define the meaning of its existence. It is the assembly of those who *perceive* what is already *true* — namely, that the Son of God has reconciled the *world* with God and that therefore his Holy Spirit does not stand still but blows where it chooses (John 3:8). Because this truth is perceived in the church, it is the assembly of those who are called to be the messengers, the missionaries in the service of God in the world.

In carrying out their mission, those who are so called take with all seriousness their confession of the Lord who *is* truly the Lord. They take it seriously, as Karl Barth said back then, in that the church practices the "solidarity of the heathen inside with the heathen outside."[24] This will result in resistance, because the people outside the church customarily do not want to be understood as heathen. These people do not, in fact, have empty hands but *full* hands, or *think* at least that they have full hands. They are people who do not wait for *us* to fill them, but rather encounter us with incomprehension or rejection because they have already filled their hands richly, with this or that religion. Perhaps they shame us with the zeal and seriousness with which they pursue their cause. Perhaps they make us a counteroffer and recommend to us the wealth of their religion. This has already so profoundly impressed and intimidated some Christians that they then can only say, No, we don't want any mission, but rather only dialogue. There are, after all, many ways to reach God. Or they wish to sate themselves on the riches of other religions — the person who can't understand that is a philistine! But one may well ask whether Christians who satiate themselves in this way do not resemble the prodigal son of Luke 15, who

---

24. Barth, "Die Theologie und die Mission in der Gegenwart," p. 102.

squandered his fortune (v. 13) and departed from his father's house. Have they forgotten that according to the biblical message there is no other way to God apart from the reverse way of God to us, the way that God has in fact already walked? For on all the other ways we find only pictures that humans have projected of themselves on the heavens, as the philosopher Feuerbach once put it.[25] The question is put to the *Christians* whether with all their openness they then *themselves* believe what the biblical witness summons them to believe: "For *God* so loved the *world* that he gave his only Son, so that everyone who believes in him may not perish but have eternal life" (John 3:16)? It is not a question of propaganda or of Christian dominion over the world. But it is permissible to ask: Can, according to Holy Scripture, the answer of the church of Christ to the religions be anything other than mission?

Yet one cannot say this without the suspicion emerging that such an undertaking could be what the sixth thesis rejects as false doctrine, an action of human self-glorification. And it is an especially stubborn evil that presents itself as a divinely legitimated "human self-glorification." There is no basis on the Christian side for the arrogance of human self-glorification. Let us, for once, not even mention the mass of Christian sins in so many areas. Basically, the source of such sins in heathen Christianity, which, according to the Bible, includes all of us, is a deep problem, and we would gain much if we were only to see it and to be disquieted by it. Heathen Christianity in our Christian territories is generally a combination, impossible on the face of it, of paganism and Christianity. That is easy to see today when at Christmas or Easter the pagan celebration begins to emancipate itself from the Christian components. The poet Friedrich Hebbel wrote back in the nineteenth century: "The most devout of Christians does not lightly / An idol break, because yet a last remnant / Of the old fear in him moves secretly / When he does see it glare."[26] When we become aware of this,

25. L. Feuerbach, *Das Wesen des Christentums* (1849; Stuttgart: Reclam UB 4571-77, 1971), pp. 46, 49; ET: *The Essence of Christianity*, trans. G. Eliot (New York: Harper, 1957), pp. 5, 9-10.

26. F. Hebbel, *Die Nibelungen: ein deutsches Trauerspiel*, Part 2, Act 2, vv. 1062-69; ET: *The Niebelungs: A Tragedy in Three Parts*, trans. H. Goldberger (London: A. Siegle, 1921), Part 2, Act 2, Scene 5, p. 47.

then we suddenly understand what the *Jew* Franz Rosenzweig once said to us Christians: We do indeed have the mission to call heathen to conversion, *but* above all else "the Christian must directly convert himself, the heathen *within himself.*"[27] Seen in that way, there are certainly very concrete grounds for the church to practice that "solidarity of the heathen inside with the heathen outside" — but to do so in the hope that the God testified to in the Bible will again care for humanity as he has cared for it already. That this hope is not in vain may be confirmed by the fact that, outside the boundaries of Christianity in the varied world of human religions, we can come across signs of the *truth* that *we* have forgotten and repressed. In one of the later sections of the *Church Dogmatics,* headed up coincidentally by the first thesis of the Barmen Declaration, Karl Barth explained that the one Word of God is testified to in truths *outside* the church.[28] These truths are witnesses of *the* truth, which is upheld against us and all people and at the same time for us and all people. They are witnesses *of* the truth that is the foundation both of the political service of God as well as of the missional sending of the church. They are witnesses *of* the truth that, according to Matthew 28, the risen Jesus Christ himself asserted and from which we and everyone else, God be thanked, live: "All authority in heaven and on earth has been given to me" (v. 18).

---

27. F. Rosenzweig, *Der Stern der Erlösung* (1921; Frankfurt am Main: Suhrkamp, 1988), p. 317; ET: *The Star of Redemption,* trans. W. W. Hallo (Notre Dame: University of Notre Dame Press, 1970), p. 285.

28. See *KD* § 69 = *CD* IV/3, 1st half, §69.